The Work-at-Home Mom's

WAHM = WORK AT HOME MOM

Guide to Home Business

Stay at Home and Make Money with WAHM.com

By Cheryl Demas

Copyright © 2000 by Cheryl Demas

Published in the United States by

Hazen Publishing, Inc., Auburn, CA

Phone: (530) 823-3659

E-Mail address: karihzn@aol.com

cheryl@wahm.com

Distributed by Sasquatch Books, Seattle, WA

ISBN 1-891506-49-8

For information regarding this book contact Kari Hazen at (530) 823-3659

Visit the WAHM website at www.wahm.com

Manufactured in the United States of America

Book Design by Mystic Design

Production by Ann Davis Production

www.wahm.com

DEDICATIONS:

Dedicated to my dad,
Allen Anderson.
No matter how many miles
separate us, I know your love
is always with me.

And to my mother-in-law,
Florence Demas.
Thank you for raising a
wonderful son.

ACKNOWLEDGMENTS

After working on my website WAHM.com for five years, I decided to take my years of experience and publish a book for mothers who, like me, want to work at home while raising their children. There were many people who made this possible. First, thanks to Karan Sims, Joanne Hahn, Sarah Ganley and Carla Massie who read the first versions of the manuscript. Thanks also to all the WAHM.com readers and on-line friends who have been so helpful. I can't possibly name you all, but I appreciate all your help, advice and friendship.

Special thanks to my husband, Mike, who makes everything possible, and to my wonderful daughters, Nicki and Dani, who make it all worthwhile.

Thanks to my publisher Kari Hazen for being both the voice of reason and a good friend.

Finally, thanks to Georgia Hughes (editor and proofreader), Ann Davis (production), Laurel Mathe at Mystic Design (art director and designer), and Angela O'Brien (proofreader) for making this book a breeze.

www.wahm.com

INTRODUCTION 3

1. WORKING MOTHERS.................................... 5
News Flash.. 6
WAHM.com Money Saving Tip: Eliminate Expenses.......... 8
A Fork in the Road.. 9
Getting Down to Business: Self-Assessment 10
It's a Mom Thing 11
WAHM.com Money Making Tip:
    Turn Your Hobby into a Business 13
The First WAHM.. 14

2. IS WORKING AT HOME RIGHT FOR YOU? 17
Profile of a WAHM 18
WAHM.com Money Making Tip: Be a Super Saleswoman .. 20
A Home Business Quiz....................................... 21
Getting Down to Business: Work-at-Home Pros and Cons 23
You Might Be a WAHM 24
WAHM.com readers: Do you ever regret your
    work-at-home decision? 25

3. CHOOSING A BUSINESS 27
What Can I Do? 28
Keys to Choosing Your Business............................ 32
WAHM.com readers: How did you choose your business?. 36
Getting Down to Business: Sample WAHM Schedules....... 38
WAHM.com Success Stories 42
I Hate Sales... 45
WAHM.com Money Making Tip:
    Choose Your Products Carefully 47
The Plate Is Hot 48
WAHM.com Scam Alert...................................... 49
WAHM.com readers: Have you ever been scammed
    by a work-at-home opportunity? 50
WAHM.com Money Making Tip: Government Contracts .. 51
But Where Are the Giraffes? 52
WAHM.com Money Making Tip: Getting Online 54

4. MAKING THE TRANSITION........................... 59
Adding a New Member to the Family...................... 60
Getting Down to Business: Choosing the Structure
    for Your Business 64
Getting Down to Business: Your Business Plan 66
Ode to an Office Chair....................................... 68
Getting Down to Business: Setting Up Your Home Office .. 69

wahm.com

TABLE OF CONTENTS

wahm.com

TABLE OF CONTENTS

WAHM.com readers: Do you have a separate space
for your office? 71

WAHM.com Time Saving Tip: Great Gadgets for WAHMs .. 72

**5. TAKING CARE OF YOUR HOME WHILE
RUNNING YOUR HOME BUSINESS** 73

Your Home and Your Business 74

WAHM.com Time-Saving Tip: Housekeeping
and Children 75

I'm a Housewife? 76

Seven Habits of Happy WAHMs 77

WAHM.com Time-Saving Tip: Scheduled Cleaning 79

The Boomerang Books 80

Getting Down to Business: Consulting 82

If Housework Brings One Closer to God, I'm in Heaven ... 83

Rules for a WAHM Home 84

WAHM.com Readers: How do you handle housekeeping? . 86

When I Get Around to it 87

Getting Down to Business: The Procrastination Problem .. 88

**6. TAKING CARE OF BUSINESS –
TAKING CARE OF YOURSELF** 89

I'm Alone in Here 90

WAHM.com Sanity Tip: Take Time for Yourself 92

Tylenol for Mom 93

WAHM.com Sanity Tip: Serve Your Community 95

Hey Dad? 96

WAHM.com Money Saving Tip: Don't Become
Your Own Best Customer 97

WAHM.com readers: How do you handle sick days? 98

Getting Down to Business: Take a Break 100

WAHM.com readers: Are you taking care of yourself? 101

WAHM.com readers: Do you dress for success or
dress to depress? 103

7. HUSBANDS AND HOME BUSINESSES 105

Husbands 106

WAHM.com Money Saving Tip: Spending Quality Time
with Your Husband Doesn't Have to Be Expensive 107

WAHM.com Time Saving Tip: Help Make Dad
Time Special 108

My Sausage 109

WAHM.com Money Making Tip: Hire Your Family 111

WAHM.com readers: Does your husband support
your business? 112

If You're on Your Own 115

8. CHILDREN AND HOME BUSINESSES 117
Mixing Children and Business 118
*WAHM.com Tip: Be Creative With Your
    Children's Activities* 120
It's a Good Thing 121
*WAHM.com Money Making Tip: Pay Attention to Your
    Customers' Interests and Hobbies* 123
The Back Burner 124
*WAHM.com Money Saving Tip: Take Advantage
    of Services in Your Community* 126
Bookstores and Alligators 127
WAHM.com Money Saving Tip: Cheap Fun 129
What's Your Title? 130
WAHM.com Time-Saving Tip: Creative Cooperation 132
Mother-Daughter Communication 133
*WAHM.com readers: What do your children think
    of your business?* 135
*WAHM.com readers: Do you have a love-hate
    relationship with your TV? Is it off-limits or
    your babysitter?* 137
*WAHM.com readers: How do you handle business
    phone calls?* 139

9. PROMOTING YOUR BUSINESS 141
Promoting Your Business, Promoting Yourself 142
What Do I Get? 144
*WAHM.com Money Making Tip: Using Press Releases
    to Promote Your Business* 146
It's All in the Packaging 148
*WAHM.com Money Making Tip: Keep Your Customers
    Happy* 150
The Grass is Always Greener–Mom? Can We Eat at
    the Neighbor's House? 151
*WAHM.com Money Making Tip: Include Your Children
    In Your Merchandising* 153
Money, Money, Money 154
*WAHM.com Money Making Tip: Use Cross-Promotion
    to Maximize Your Ad Dollars* 156
Good Bagels 157
*WAHM.com readers: How do you promote your business?
    What works best for you?* 159

10. MOTIVATION 161
Oprah Calling 162
Oprah Called! 164

wahm.com

TABLE OF CONTENTS

WAHM.com Money Making Tip:
   Visualize Your Success 166
I Love the Talking 167
Be the Bunny 168
WAHM.com Money Making Tip: Telecommuting 170
A Gift for You 171
Better Than Sex 173
WAHM.com Money Making Tip: Barter 175
Report Card Time 176
WAHM.com readers: Do you ever get down in the dumps?
   How do you stay motivated? 177

11. HOW DO YOU SPELL SUCCESS? 179
New Year's Resolutions 180
Getting Down to Business–Financing Your Business 182
Big, Bigger, ??? 183
WAHM.com Readers: How do you define success? 184

12. AND FINALLY 185
WAHM.com Readers: What is the best business advice
   you've ever received? 186
My Advice to All WAHMs 188

APPENDIX A: WORK-AT-HOME IDEAS 190

APPENDIX B: DIRECT SALES COMPANIES 192

APPENDIX C 204
WAHM.com readers: What would you tell someone
   who's not online yet? How has WAHM.com helped
   you and your business? 205

APPENDIX D: SAMPLE PRESS RELEASE 208

IS EVERY DAY...

"Take Our Children to Work Day"?

ARE THERE...

Legos under your desk?

IS YOUR...

coffeepot the most-used
appliance in your home?

THEN, YOU'RE A...

WAHM, and this
is your book!

www.wahm.com

Introduction

In 1994, my then seven-year-old daughter, Nicki, was diagnosed with diabetes. That was Tuesday. On Friday, our second daughter, Dani, was born. I had been a traditional "working mother" up to that time. I had always enjoyed my career as an engineer, but within that life-changing week, my husband and I decided I would stay at home with the girls. Even as much as I wanted to be home with my girls, it wasn't an easy decision. Once a budget is set up based on two incomes, it is difficult to convert back to one. I also derived a great deal of my identity and self-esteem from my career.

But we made the decision and I started using the Internet to research diabetes information for my daughter. I was frustrated and offended by all the work-at-home schemes and scams aimed at moms. There seemed to be a general attitude that if a mother chooses to stay at home with her children, she must not have any marketable skills or education. Because of my engineering background, I chose website design as my home business. And, because working from home was such a good solution for my family and me, I also started a website: WAHM.com–the online magazine for Work-at-Home Moms (WAHMs).

I focus on moms because, being one myself, it is what I know best. I also think work-at-home moms face unique challenges not shared by our male counterparts. We are asked to watch our friends' children, bake cupcakes for the kindergarten class, pick up the neighbors' kids from school, be den mothers and troop leaders. We are at home, after all.

Even though women working from home may be expected to do things all mothers do, they can also operate successful—and diverse—businesses. Since starting my website in 1995, I've heard from hundreds of thousands of intelligent, well-educated women. They have chosen to leave the "traditional workplace" to be at home with their children. They have chosen to be full-time caregivers for their children; yet they still want, and need, to work and make money. A few of them are making a lot of money, enough to support their families. Most of them, through reducing their expenses and the income from their work-at-home businesses (from $100 to $1000 per month), are making enough to be able to stay at home with their children–their number one priority.

Through the years, I've learned a lot from my readers, and I've learned a lot from my mistakes. This book is a lighthearted look at the work-at-home lifestyle. It is a collection of my columns and cartoons, describing things I've learned and experienced these past five years, combined with practical advice and Money Making and Money Saving Tips. Because the best advice usually comes from the "voice of experience," I've also included quotations and advice I've collected from WAHM.com readers.

My purpose with this book isn't to try to convince you that you should stay home with your kids or that you will be happier staying home with your kids. Working at home may not be for everyone, and it isn't always easy, but it certainly has been worth it for me!

I hope you will read this book as you start your business and return to it from time to time as your business grows. Pick it up when you need support or when you need to reaffirm your decision to work at home.

If you want to work-at-home, I want to help you succeed.

CHAPTER ONE

Working Mothers

I'm tired. Tired of the mommy wars and all of the debates over working moms vs. stay-at-home moms. I don't care how many studies I read that tell me child care won't harm my children, they won't change my mind. I love being home. If you're trying to decide if home is the place for you, or whether or not you really want to work at home, this is for you.

News Flash

Recently, our local news led with the story: "Working moms, lose your guilt. Children are not harmed by child care."

Funny, but I don't think this good news is going to send a huge rush of moms into the workplace.

I don't know about other families or the thousands of children studied. I only know about my own children and my family. My kids are happy at home, I'm happy, and my husband's happy. When I was working full-time, home was not a relaxing place to be. A sick child

brought panic and frantic juggling of schedules. An unplanned business trip threw our lives into turmoil. Neither my husband nor I could really devote ourselves to either our careers or our family because we were always being pulled in different directions. We were ruled by rigid schedules and conflicted loyalties.

The problem I see with these studies and the ensuing debates is the assumption that no woman in her right mind would actually choose to "make the sacrifice" and leave the mental stimulation of the workplace simply to take care of her children. Do you get the feeling that we're being told that as long as we have the proof that our kids aren't harmed by child care, there shouldn't be anyone who chooses, actually prefers, to stay at home and take care of her children?

Staying at home with my kids isn't a sacrifice for me; it is a joy. Sure, I still have other interests, things I like to do that don't include the kids. That's one of the reasons why I have a home business. But nothing is more important to me than being here for my kids. I wouldn't trade these days for anything–money, status, titles–none of it means as much to me as my main title, Mom. And judging by the number of visitors to WAHM.com and the mail I receive, there are a lot of other moms who agree.

This may not be your experience, and I'm not trying to tell anyone what he or she should do, or presume to know what will make anyone else happy. I just know what makes me happy, and that's being home with my kids.

I guess "Moms Love Being Home with Their Kids" just doesn't make for a very exciting headline.

MONEY SAVING

TIP!

Eliminate Expenses

Everyone knows "a penny saved is a penny earned." If you're working away from home, think about the expenses eliminated if you decide to stay at home. Add up the cost of your work: clothing, meals away from home, convenience foods, child care, car insurance, gasoline. By eliminating these expenses from your budget, you're already making money before you even start working at home.

Approximate Monthly Expenses

This is just a sample comparison of the extra annual expenses in the following situations. Depending on your individual circumstances, such as the ages and number of your children, your geographic area, your career, and your home business, these numbers will vary. Use this as a guideline to calculate your own expenses.

Many of your at-home business expenses, including purchasing a computer, cellular phone, telephone service, office supplies, internet connection, legal advice, and accounting advice, may be tax deductible. Consult your accountant and check out the IRS's website for small businesses: www.irs.gov/bus_info.

COMPARE EXPENSES

Work-at-Home			Work Away from Home		
Expense	Sample $	Your $	Expense	Sample $	Your $
Home office wardrobe	$0		Professional wardrobe	$2000	
Meals away from home	$0		Meals away from home	$1200	
Gas	$0		Gas	$2400	
Office supplies and general business expenses	$1200		Office supplies	$0	
Time with your children	*Priceless*		Child care	$6000	
Other				Other	
Other				Other	
Net savings	$10,400				

A Fork in the Road

In the past, we were told that we would be able to have a career and raise a family. We could have it all. We believed it. We received our degrees, embarked on our careers, and then we had our children. And many of us discovered that if this is what having it all is like, maybe we don't want it all, after all.

I came to a fork in the road a few years ago and decided that I would follow my heart, following the "motherhood" route. I'm thankful that working at home has allowed me to continue working, because I actually enjoy work, too. However, as much as I like my home business, I can't imagine a job that could give me the satisfaction I get from raising my girls.

And that's the good news. I've found that motherhood isn't a one-way street. I'm getting back so much more from my role as "mom" than I'm giving. I know people always say that being a parent is the most difficult job there is, and there are challenges, but I can't imagine anything else I'd rather be doing.

My five-year-old summed it up for me as she was getting ready for bed the other night. She asked me, "Mom, what would you do without me?" I thought about our bedtime stories, hugs, "I love Mommy" notes, and the laughs we have together. That night, as I watched her sleep, I thought the same thing myself, what would I do without them?

GETTING DOWN TO BUSINESS

Self-Assessment

As you're making the decision whether or not to stay at home or start a home business, use this self-assessment exercise to clarify your thoughts. First, answer these general questions to help you think about the reasons that you want to work at home.

- If I choose to work at home, what is the best thing that could happen?
- What is the worst thing that could happen?
- Why do I really want to do this?
- What things are stopping me from working at home?
- How will my family and I benefit if I start a home business?
- Will my family suffer in any way if I work at home?
- Will my family benefit in any way if I continue working away from home?
- Will we suffer in any way if I continue to work away from home?

To help you determine if you are well suited for working at home, ask yourself these questions:

- Do I have the self-discipline necessary to work on my own?
- Will I be able to handle the isolation that comes with working on my own?
- Will I be able to work efficiently and keep my business paperwork organized?
- Can I afford to get along without an income until my business is established?
- Can I fit regular working hours into my daily schedule?
- Do I have a network of friends and family who will support my business and me?
- Am I willing to get the training I need, take classes, and attend seminars that are necessary to run my business?

It's a Mom Thing

I have tried in the past to explain to childless friends why I left a good, high-paying job to work at home, to stay at home with my kids. I've never really felt that I could adequately describe the reasons I want to be home with my girls. I've never felt that I had successfully convinced anyone that I'm doing what I really want to do. They still seem to think that I'm sacrificing something, or missing out, just so I don't have to put my kids in child care.

A few years ago, my daughter made a huge tissue paper Mother's Day carnation corsage for me. She presented it to me on Mother's Day morning, and of course expected that I would wear it all day. And I did. I wore it to church, to breakfast, to the mall. From other mothers I received smiles and knowing glances; from non-mothers, I received stares and curious looks. I could tell they were wondering what would possess me to attach several square feet of multicolored tissue paper to my chest. I overheard one of the young salesclerks at the mall say to a colleague as they walked away, "It must be a Mom Thing."

MOTHER'S DAY: THE *ONE* DAY I GET THE RECOGNITION I SO RICHLY DESERVE!

I knew they could never understand, so I didn't even try to explain. But after I thought about it, I decided she was right. It is a "Mom Thing." Before I was a mom, there was no way I could have understood it either.

Before I had children of my own, I always liked kids, but I was always glad to get away from them, too. I assumed it would be the same when I had children of my own. I would enjoy my time with them, but then I would need to "get away" and have time for myself. So when I was pregnant, I imagined that after a short maternity leave, I would continue on with my forty to fifty hour work week without a hitch. I was caught completely off guard by my desire to stay home with my children. These aren't like those other kids, the ones I could take or leave. These are my kids! Leaving them with someone else is like leaving part of myself behind. I just couldn't do it. And that's why I'm working from home. It is the only way I'd have it.

My childless, career-minded friends might not understand why I'm doing this, and I shouldn't expect them to–anymore than I would expect the girls at the mall to understand why I would wear that giant corsage. It's just a "Mom Thing."

Turn Your Hobby into a Business

If you like crafts, here's one way you can turn your hobby into a Money Making venture. Since we know that homemade gifts are always the most cherished gifts a parent receives, create a kid's craft workshop before holidays. Make flyers advertising the workshop. Take advantage of any free advertising opportunities you can find, such as advertising at child care centers, preschools, local elementary schools, and community bulletin boards. See if a local art teacher or art center might want to get involved. Make sure you charge enough per child to pay for the materials, advertising, and your time. Build a mailing list from each craft workshop, so you can build a customer database and get repeat business.

At the workshop, you can help the children make handprint heart boxes for Valentine's Day, self-portraits and custom frames for Mother's and Father's Day, and personalized ornaments for other holidays. Children will have a good time and their parents will actually be surprised when they open their gifts.

MONEY MAKING

TIP!

The First WAHM

"What doesn't last in any human society known to anthropology is to have women working away from their families. Now that the technology is setting them free, women are leading the movement back to the home, and men are following them."–George Gilder.

In the history of anthropology? Can that be true? Let's take a peek into Christy Cave-Dwellers diary:

JUST "BURP" IT LIKE THIS AND YOUR SABER-TOOTH TACOS WILL STAY FRESH FOR DAYS!

THE FIRST WAHM

Dear Diary: I killed my first saber-toothed tiger today. I'm proud of the fact that I can hunt along with the men. This new freedom to do what I want to do is soooo liberating.

Dear Diary: Yesterday after dinner, Jimmy from the other village knocked me over the head and dragged me off to his cave. I'm so happy.

Dear Diary: Now that Jimmy Junior is on the way, we've decided that I will continue to hunt as I did before Jim dragged me to his cave. Linda, one of the women who stays at her cave all day, will take care of Junior while I'm away. I don't know how she can stand being in that cave all day. I need more mental stimulation than that!

Dear Diary: Things aren't working out exactly as I had planned. When I'm hunting, I miss Junior more than you can imagine. Then when I get home, I still have more work to do. All Big Jim does is complain that the cave is always a mess. Who has time to do everything?

Dear Diary: All of the extra food we get from my hunting trips goes to pay Linda for watching Jim Junior. What's the point of being away from home all day if I have nothing to show for it?

Dear Diary: Margo and Lisa, the other "hunting mothers" both say I'm helping Junior by showing him that women can be hunters, too. I think all he's learning is that Linda is there to hug him when he's sad and I'm not.

Dear Diary: There's a woman here in the village who is always talking, telling everyone what to do: Dr. Laura Schlessrubble. She says I should be home with Junior. She says he needs his mom more than he needs fresh meat every single night. I agree with her. Some of the people here think she talks too much, but I think she may have a future in the talking business.

Dear Diary: I decided to quit hunting today. We will get by somehow. Margo called me a cave-wife; I don't really care for that. I'm thinking of doing some kind of work from home. I notice a lot of the food we bring home spoils before we can eat it. If only we had some kind of containers that would keep the food fresh . . . Hmmm I wonder . . .?

CHAPTER TWO

Is Working at Home Right for You?

The home business lifestyle isn't for everyone. There are several things to consider before you begin. Will you miss the chats with your coworkers? Can you discipline yourself to sit down and work on a beautiful day? Can you get along without a regular paycheck, at least while you're establishing the business? Remember that taking care of your home and your family is a full-time job in itself. Add a home business to the mix and something has got to give. This chapter will give you an idea if your personality and your home and family are suited for the work-at-home lifestyle.

Profile of a WAHM

I've been amazed by the variety of people I've met since I started WAHM.com. There are work-at-home moms all over the world, doing every imaginable type of work at home. They live in big cities and in rural areas. There are married WAHMs, single WAHMs, and Grandma WAHMs. Yet, even with all the diversity, successful WAHMs seem to share several personality traits. I've combined these traits to come up with the following profile of the typical WAHM.

Entrepreneurial Spirit

The typical WAHM has a strong entrepreneurial personality. She may have been the first child in her neighborhood to set up a lemonade stand in the summer or organize a used-toy sale with her friends. She is always looking for a new way to make money. She is energized by the idea of starting something from scratch and thrives on the excitement of a new business venture.

Resilience

The typical WAHM knows that ups and downs are part of doing business and she doesn't let the bad times keep her down for long. Although she knows enough to cut her losses and move on when it becomes apparent that a particular venture isn't going to work out, she doesn't let a setback keep her from pursuing her work at home dreams. She applies the lessons she learns from failures to her next venture. So even if her first attempts at a home business don't live up to her expectations, she perseveres and keeps trying.

Dedication

Dedication to her business is another trait of the typical WAHM. She is a hard worker and is willing to go the extra mile to make her business stand out from the rest. If it means late nights and early mornings, or carrying samples in and out of demonstrations, she is willing to do whatever it takes. She is dedicated to her business and she keeps working to make it a success.

Creativity

The typical WAHM is creative. She sees a business opportunity around every corner. Since she doesn't have a lot of role models for her work-at-home lifestyle, she has to be creative to adapt her schedule and environment to her unique situation and to the changing needs of her business and family.

Independence

The typical WAHM is independent. She is able to work on her own and she has the self-discipline needed to meet deadlines and work when no one is standing over her.

Realistic Attitude

The successful WAHM may have big goals and dreams, but she also has a realistic vision of what she will be able to accomplish with her home businesses. She looks at the time and resources she has available and makes a realistic plan.

Desire

Last but not least, the typical WAHM has a strong desire to work at home. She knows that she wants to be at home and take care of her children, yet she still wants to work and make money. She is motivated to succeed, and she has faith in herself.

Are You a WAHM?

Does this sound like you? Do you have the entrepreneurial spirit, resilience, dedication, creativity, independence, realistic attitude, and desire to be a work-at-home mom? If you're not sure, make a gradual transition into working at home. If you think this is what you want to do, but you're scared or unsure, start slowly. You don't have to approach your home business like a bungee jump into the unknown. Begin part time; work at home while you keep your traditional job. You may even find that being a part-time WAHM works best for you. As I said, WAHMs are all different. You will find the mix that works best for you.

MONEY MAKING

TIP!

Be a Super Saleswoman

- Have you heard the story of the two shoe salesmen who were sent to a foreign country? The first one calls the home office and says, "Bring me home, nobody here wears shoes!" The second calls the home office and says, "Send more salespeople, nobody here wears shoes!" If you're considering sales, find a niche. Meet a need that isn't being met in your community.

- So you don't get discouraged, use this tip for getting through rejection. Write the word "No" on a piece of paper 99 times. Now write "Yes" once. Every time you approach someone with your business proposal or sales pitch and they say "No" cross off one of the "No's" on your list. Now you're that much closer to your "Yes"! This way, even rejection brings you closer to your goal.

- If you are going into a sales-related business, realize that rejection will be part of it, and plan for the time you will need to make contacts. For example, you may need to schedule uninterrupted time for some tasks, such as phone calls. Plan to make your calls during nap times, or while your children are at school. Schedule your calling time and then do it. It is essential to the success of your business.

- Learn to use the Internet to your advantage. Put as much of your product information online as you can and then use email to answer customers' questions. Email can be answered at any time of the day, and you don't need to eliminate background noise to type an email.

A Home Business Quiz

I'm often asked, "How can I tell if I have what it takes to be a work-at-home mom?" In an attempt to help you undecided moms, I've created a little quiz that will give you some insight into the life of a work-at-home mom. Imagine yourself in the following situations:

1. You inherit $1000 from a long lost relative. You think:

  a) Great! Now I can take that vacation I've always dreamed of.

  b) I could sure use a new wardrobe.

  c) Woohoo! Now I can buy a laser printer!

2. You get a new computer, now you can:

  a) Finally get your recipes organized.

  b) Learn to play one of those multi-player Internet games.

  c) Set up your business website.

WHICH MOM HAS A HOME BUSINESS?

3. The laundry and dirty dishes are piled up, you have a job deadline looming, you:

  a) Drop everything and clean, clean, clean.

  b) Try to finish the job, but you just can't concentrate until the dishes are done.

  c) Finish the job; the dishes will still be there when you're done.

4. It's 1:00 a.m., you are most happy if you are:

  a) Sleeping.

  b) Out on the town.

  c) Preparing invoices.

5. When you see a successful businesswoman, do you think:

a) I am so jealous of her.

b) Why is she wearing those shoes with that dress?

c) I could do that!

6. When you drive into work, do you think:

a) Phew, I'm glad to get away from my family.

b) I'm sure the socialization at child care is good for my children.

c) I can't do this anymore.

If you answered "c" to all of the above questions, congratulations! I'd say you have what it takes to be a work-at-home mom.

Note from Cheryl: If anyone chose "a" on question number 3, I'd like to give you my address because I could really use someone like you at my house.

Work-at-Home Pros and Cons

The reality of working at home is often different than the TV commercials we see. You know the ones, Mom is attending a virtual board meeting in her bunny slippers while her toddler plays contentedly in the background.

Here are some of the realistic pros and cons of working at home:

WEIGH THE REALITIES	
PROS	**CONS**
You can work in comfortable clothes.	You may end up wearing frumpy sweat suits all the time.
You are free to set your own hours; therefore you will have more freedom to attend field trips and school plays.	If you don't schedule your time carefully, your business may take over all of your free time.
You are the primary caretaker for your children.	You might find it difficult to fit work in with all of your other duties.
You'll get a self-esteem boost from running your own business.	Others might not take you seriously because you don't have a "real job."
There will be no holes in your resume, if and when you decide to return to the traditional workplace.	You have to pay for your own training and education.
You are paid directly for the work you do.	You may not get a steady paycheck.
You set an example for your children. They learn about business and the entrepreneurial lifestyle.	Your children may see the bad side of business, too; the stress and the headaches. When you work at home, you can't use your commute time to decompress.
You learn about and stay up-to-date on business regulations and tax laws that relate to home businesses.	The paperwork can be overwhelming.
You are your own boss.	You can't call in sick.

You Might Be a WAHM

If you call four hours of uninterrupted sleep a good night's rest . . .
you might be a WAHM

If you synchronize your working hours with the Blue's Clues TV schedule . . .
you might be a WAHM

If the corporate cafeteria is your refrigerator . . .
you might be a WAHM

If you type email while nursing . . .
you might be a WAHM

If your husband thinks a home-cooked meal is re-heated Taco Bell . . .
you might be a WAHM

If your idea of a great anniversary gift is a new laser printer . . .
you might be a WAHM

If your work wardrobe consists of jeans, T-shirts, and slippers . . .
you might be a WAHM

If you wish days were 36 hours long . . .
you might be a WAHM

If you mark the change of seasons by whether or not the UPS man is wearing shorts . . .
you might be a WAHM

If you spend your free time wondering what it would be like to have free time . . .
you might be a WAHM

If you consider the play land at McDonald's an off-site meeting facility . . .
you might be a WAHM

If your children tell their friends, "No, my mom doesn't work, she takes care of us" . . .
you might be a WAHM

Do you ever regret your work-at-home decision?

No, no, no! I had first started working at home with a computer company that I worked for "before kids" at their office. I have since resigned from the company, and I am now looking for something new to do. I am having a problem accepting any job that requires me to leave my virtual office. I am comfortable here—I am my own boss, and most importantly, my children are raised My Way! We get many compliments about how well behaved our children are. I can only thank my husband—and myself, not a nanny or babysitter.

There are days when I wish I was relaxing on the beach, but never a day when I wished I was back in the workplace. My kids are the main reason I work from home, but I'm happy that I don't have to deal with office politics and I like running my own show.

I have never regretted my decision. My only regret is that I didn't start working from home until my firstborn was 18 months old. I feel I missed a lot, especially now that I have another child and can compare notes. The only thing I would do differently is start working from home sooner.

From the moment we decided to have a child, the decision was made that one of us would stay home. My job involved travel so I won and have never regretted our decision one second! My at-home business is very important and it's expanding as my son grows (now age five and in school). Now I have more time to devote to the business. However, my primary job is to help my son reach his potential to become a great human and being here for him. My second job is the business, and the third is to teach my husband how to use the washing machine.

Yes and no. I get so tired sometimes, I think it might be easier in some ways to go back to a regular job. But I know that with the type of personality I have, it's difficult to be happy with a nine-to-five job. I've certainly done it before, and done it well, but I find it stifling.

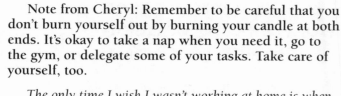

READERS

Note from Cheryl: Remember to be careful that you don't burn yourself out by burning your candle at both ends. It's okay to take a nap when you need it, go to the gym, or delegate some of your tasks. Take care of yourself, too.

The only time I wish I wasn't working at home is when I'm running into deadlines and I'm wearing too many hats at once. You know, the baby's sick, I have a deadline, the car broke down, the phone's ringing off the hook, the dog just peed on the carpet, and my hubby calls to say he's bringing someone home. I miss being able to delegate, but not enough to go back to work on the outside!

Note from Cheryl: Remember what it was like when you were working away from home: your baby would still be sick, the car would still break down, but you would have a boss to deal with, too. You can still delegate, but you may have to be a little more creative. Turn on the answering machine, tell your husband he needs to bring food home with him when he brings a guest, and the kids will have to clean up after the dog. You can also delegate by making arrangements with other work-at-home moms. Set up a network of women with whom you can exchange child care when you have a deadline, or carpool with other moms to pick up the kids after school.

CHAPTER THREE

Choosing a Business

So, you've decided that working at home is for you. Now you just have to figure out what to do. There are several factors to consider, including your skills, how much time you will have to devote to your business, and how much money you will need to make. This chapter will give you some ideas and help you answer those questions.

What Can I Do?

I'm asked this question more than any other: "I want to work at home but I don't know what to do. What kind of job can I do from home?" The quick answer is, you can do almost anything from home. I believe the Internet is the single greatest factor that is allowing more moms to be able to work at home today. Now, through email and websites, we can communicate with people all over the world, at any time of the day or night. We can display our products online, contact clients through email, conduct meetings in chat rooms, and even find jobs online. There are so many choices, the real challenge is narrowing down all the opportunities and choosing the one that is right for you. It's almost easier to name the jobs that can't be done from home. Okay, so you can't be a bus driver, but I think you might be surprised by the number of businesses that can be run from home.

SURE I'D LIKE TO MAKE MONEY AT HOME, I JUST DON'T WANT TO <u>WORK</u> AT HOME!

The first thing I always recommend is that moms think about their skills and interests. Have you heard the expression, "Do what you love and the money will follow"? Well, it's no guarantee, but if you do what you love, and you are truly devoted to making your business a success, and you are very good at what you do, you will have a much better chance of success. If you choose a business simply because someone has told you it will make money, but your heart isn't in it, success is not likely.

If you would like to continue working with your current employer, perhaps on a freelance basis, see if there is a way you can do your work from home, at least part-time. Is it possible to do your work remotely from your home office?

If you're ready to begin a business of your own, the list of businesses in appendix A will give you some ideas. Since starting WAHM.com, I've been amazed by the variety of work moms are doing at home. I know one soccer mom who sells ad space on her minivan! Appendix A doesn't contain just a list of ideas. I've met Moms doing these businesses from home, right now. Some of these jobs are common, and some are unique. Some have six-figure income potential and some bring in just a little extra spending money. You have to evaluate your needs and find the business that fits your own unique situation.

Some home businesses require that you spend a few hours away from home each day. These are probably best suited for moms with older children, so away-from-home time can be scheduled during school hours. If you can be more flexible, you can schedule your away-from-home time for nights and weekends when your husband is home or another family member is available to help.

For some careers, writing for example, it's easy to see how you can transfer your skills to a home business. For others, however, you may have to be a little more creative. Here are some ideas for careers whose home business applications may not be as obvious:

If you are currently:	Some jobs you can do at home:
Accountant	• Tax Preparation
	• Small business accounting and bookkeeping services
Administrative Assistant	• Secretarial support for small businesses
	• Desktop publishing services
	• Typing/word processing services
	• Prepare resumes for college students
Attorney	• Business consulting and incorporation
	• Freelance writing on legal issues
	• Trademarks
	• Wills and trusts

Engineer	• Contract engineering work
	• Software support for small businesses
	• Freelance programming
	• Computer training
	• Website design
Librarian	• Information retrieval
	• Internet information searches
	• Book review columnist or website publisher
Marketing	• Public relations
	• Copy writing
	• Marketing plan preparation
	• Event planning
Nurse	• Personalized weight loss consulting
	• Teaching childbirth classes
	• Lactation consultant
	• Review charts for insurance companies
	• Home healthcare
	• Nutritional supplements or vitamin sales
Office Manager	• Professional organizer
	• Bookkeeping
	• Virtual office manager
Retail Saleswoman	• Direct sales (see appendix B)
Teacher	• Tutor
	• Provide classes for homeschool students, evaluate student's writing
	• Write curriculum for home school students
	• Teach standardized test preparation classes

Things to Keep in Mind

- How much time do I have to devote to my business?
- How much money will I need to start this business?
- How will I fit this business into my schedule?
- Will I need to buy a computer?
- What other office supplies will I need?
- How will I get start-up money for the business: savings, loans?
- Will I have free time to make sales calls or attend meetings without my children?
- Am I comfortable marketing and promoting myself?
- How can I transfer my skills to this business?
- Can I handle the stress, deadlines and do it all well?
- Am I able to let my housework slide if I need to in order to complete my work?

Keys to Choosing Your Business

What things do you love to do?

What are your interests? How do you spend your free time? Is this a business you can discuss with excitement with the people you meet? Can you wake up each morning, enthusiastic to start the day?

Believe me, your home business can become part of each waking moment–and even your sleep. I have a friend who decided it was time to dump her home business when she started having nightmares of being buried alive in her products. She has since chosen another business, selling products she loves. So far, she's been sleeping peacefully. Her only business-related dreams are of the tropical islands that she will visit because she has earned such a high home-business income.

Consider your personality. If you're an artistic introvert, a sales position may not be the best choice. And if you love to be out talking to people all day, computer programming probably isn't the best choice for you.

How much time are you willing to devote to your business?

Are you looking for a part-time business that may make a little extra money? Or are you looking for a full-time business that will be your ticket to fame and fortune?

Look at your schedule first. Consider the amount of time you will realistically be able to work, and then decide how much and what kind of work you will be able to do. You don't want to start a business, sign contracts with eight clients, and then realize that you can't possibly get it all done.

Have you decided to work from home so you can be there for your children? Then you may need to be flexible with your time, and you may not want to choose a business that will require your attention at any and all hours, night and day. How many hours a day will you be able to work? Will you work only while your children are sleeping, or just during school hours? I choose to work on my website mostly in the early morning hours before everyone gets up, and again after the kids are in bed. This works for me but may not be the best solution for you. It may be a good idea to start slowly and gradually devote more time to your business as you and your family adjust, especially if you have very small children. If you start out trying to work ten hours a day, you're likely to burn out before you even get your business off the ground.

On the other hand, if you decide you only want to work a few hours each week, you can't realistically expect that your business will make you a millionaire. While there are always stories of someone who "makes it big" with minimum time and effort, the reality is that behind most successful people are years of long hours and hard work.

Do you have experience in this business?

Most people find success in a business where they have experience. You don't necessarily have to bring your current job home, but you may be able to find a way to adapt your current occupation to your home business. For example, some nurses start home health care businesses and some teachers become home tutors.

If converting your current job is not possible and you've found a business that suits you, talk to as many people as you can to get a feeling for what running your business will really be like. You will find most people will be happy to discuss their business with you. If you need to refresh your skills, check out your local college or community college for classes.

A mom I know with a background in early childhood education chose to become a sales representative selling educational products for young children. Because of her education and because she has three boys under age five, the business fits her lifestyle and background perfectly.

She has been able to use her knowledge of early child-hood development in her presentations. Her workshops for child care professionals show them the benefits of using the products in their curriculum.

Can you realistically make money in this business?

I know a lot of women who have invested hours of their time and energy making craft items or sewing only to realize that they would have to charge a prohibitively high price for their creations to make up for the time they have devoted. Do the math, and ask questions. Just because you've heard of someone making $10,000 a month in a particular business, that doesn't guarantee that you will see the same results.

Find out how long it will take to start earning income. How much money will you have to invest? How much of your time will you have to invest? Will you have to pay for occasional child care when you have to meet with clients? It may be possible, but again, do the math.

Can you run this business from your home?

Are there zoning restrictions in your community that would prohibit you from running your business? Some areas place limits on the number of customers or clients that may visit your home each day. There may be restrictions on advertising, and manufacturing, in your neighborhood.

You will want to check with your community's county or city office and see if there are restrictions regarding the type of business you are considering before you get too far into the process of choosing. It would be a shame to become enthusiastic about a new business idea only to find out that you won't be able to run the business from home.

You must also consider if your family will be supportive of your new business endeavor. Will your business take over the garage or a spare bedroom? Butterfly ranching may sound good on paper, but will your children be willing to give up their playroom to make room for the butterflies?

Will your business take over your whole house? I know of a mom whose publishing business grew and grew to a point where her supplies were occupying every bit of free space. She finally made the decision to move her business to outside office space for the sake of her sanity and her marriage. Discuss these issues with your family and make sure you all agree and are committed to the business.

Don't be afraid to change your mind.
If your business isn't working for you, or if you're not happy with your choice, it's okay to try something else. Many successful business people didn't find success with the first business they started. That's okay. My friend who sells educational products tried two other home businesses, but because she was never passionate about the products, she wasn't very good at sharing the business with others.

Now she says she doesn't think she could ever go back to the traditional workplace. She says, "I have been home for five years and love the freedom to make my own decisions, grow my business how I choose, and arrange my day my way. I love my home and feel most comfortable here."

Good luck in your search for your perfect home business. Hopefully, you too will soon be saying, "I love my home and my home business!"

How did you choose your business?

I answered an employment ad in our local paper for some-one to do medical transcription work at home. As for my sideline business, I discovered it online. I had been a customer of a clothing website for several months. One day, I went to the site and it was closed. I loved the idea of the business so much that I offered to buy it from the previous owner.

It kind of just happened to me. I knew that I wanted and needed to do something to make money from my home. When my husband and I bought a computer in 1997, I was determined that the way I would work at home would be with my computer. Now that I'm doing website design, I find that I love being on my computer and working on my web pages. Although it took me until this year to actually make money, it was well worth the wait.

Note from Cheryl: It is rare for a business to show a profit immediately. Plan for this when you begin. Either get started while you are still working outside the home or budget for your startup phase.

My business is information retrieval and it fits my pro-fessional credentials. I was a school librarian for five and a half years. This idea hit me over the head after several people requested that I find information for them.

I am still looking for the right business. Starting last year, I tried a sales business. However, I found out that I really do hate sales. And I didn't make money at it but I did get good tax breaks and my own products at discount. On the other hand, I'm also running my own home-based freelance typing/computer consulting business. It has its ups and downs. It is getting better the more I try to organize my time and myself, which is something (I have to give credit where credit is due) I learned from the training I received from the sales company I was recruited into. So it wasn't a total loss.

I found my current freelance job through a referral from a friend. She knew of someone who needed graphics help and recommended me. I tried one other home business and it didn't work because the lead times for projects were too tight. As a WAHM I need at least 24 hours and this particular business wanted projects completed within hours. With my schedule, that's just not possible.

Note from Cheryl: This is why I recommend WAHMs consider their schedules first, and then choose their business, not the other way around.

I've tried five different home businesses. My sponsors were expecting me to make a certain amount each month and were not pleased when I was not able to do so. Family is more important than any job. I have since started another sales business and quit one of my two part-time jobs. I'm working around my family's activities to make this one work. I hope I'll be able to quit my other part-time job soon.

Note from Cheryl: If you are joining a network marketing or MLM company, question other people in the business, not just your sponsors. Your sponsors often have their own interests in mind when they are recruiting you because they will earn a percentage of your sales. Someone who has nothing to gain if you join or don't join the company is more likely to give you honest answers to your questions.

I tried a craft business and two network marketing businesses before I started my present business. Now, the primary services I offer are marketing and stock photography. The craft business (sewing little girl's dresses) didn't work for me because I found I liked creating one-of-a-kind dresses and not several hundred of the same things. The repetition nearly killed me. Both network marketing companies are reputable, but I found I wanted to sell my products rather than someone else's. I wanted to sell something I created rather than fulfill someone else's dream. I finally learned to do what I love rather than what I could. Now, when I work, I have trouble stopping because I'm having too much fun. Thank goodness my daughter's presence keeps reminding me why I started this business to begin with—so I, and not a stranger could be the one to raise her.

Sample WAHM Schedules

Joan is married and has two school-age children, ages seven and nine. She is a freelance writer. Joan is paid between $100 and $1000 for each article she sells. She also writes a weekly newspaper column for which she is paid $150 each week. She typically works seven to nine hours a day and gets seven hours of sleep a night.

5:00–7:00	Joan's up and working
7:00–9:00	Get kids up, make breakfast, showers, kids off to school
9:00–2:00	Work
2:00–6:00	After school activities, errands, chores, homework, play time, get dinner ready, get everything ready for tomorrow
6:00–7:00	Dad's home, family dinner time
7:00–9:00	Dad time: more homework, bath time, bedtime story; Joan occasionally works during this time too, depending on her workload
9:00	Kids' bedtime
10:00	Joan's bedtime

Jane is a married mom with two school-age sons and an infant daughter. She works from home part-time doing programming for her former employer. Considered an independent contractor, she is paid $45 per hour. Her modem connects to her employer's computer, and she communicates with her co-workers through email. Her work is project based, so it's not critical that she is available all day, and she is able to do a lot of her work at night. While she attends on site meetings once a week, her boys are in school and her mother-in-law cares for her baby daughter. Jane sometimes works on the weekends to finish projects. She works an average of four hours a day and gets eight hours of sleep a night.

6:00–8:30	Everyone is up, gets the boys dressed, fed and off to school
8:30–10:00	Baby and Mom time
10:00–12:00	Baby's morning nap; Jane works
12:00–2:00	Jane runs errands when needed, more baby and Mom time
2:00–5:30	Boys are home from school; errands, chores, homework, activities, and dinner preparation
5:30–6:30	Dinner time
7:00	Baby is in bed, Dad spends time with the boys
7:00–9:00	Jane works
9:00	Bedtime stories and bedtime for the boys
10:00	Bedtime for Jane

GETTING DOWN TO BUSINESS

Lena, a single mom, lives with her parents and her two-year-old son. She has a degree in graphic design and works exclusively on the Internet, designing websites and graphics for small businesses. She bills $50 per hour for design work and $25 per hour for site maintenance. She also does site promotion for which she charges a flat fee of $100. For this, she submits the site to search sites, sends press releases announcing the site to local media, and works with other related sites to exchange links. Her mother works full-time, but she is available to care for Jason each morning. Lena works six hours a day and gets seven hours of sleep a night.

6:00–8:30	Lena works; her mother cares for her son when he wakes up in the morning, gets him dressed, and makes breakfast
8:30–8:00	Lena spends the rest of her day caring for her son; she checks her email when she can during the day, while Jason naps or when he is playing on his own
8:00–11:00	Lena works again after Jason is in bed
11:00	Bedtime

Amy telecommutes for an insurance company. She is married and has two school-age daughters. She has to be available to answer phone calls from 10:00 to 3:00 each day, with an hour break at lunch. Amy's hours are very predictable. She works four hours a day and typically gets eight hours of sleep a night. When she started telecommuting just one day a week for a trial period of six months, Amy was determined to make her telecommuting arrangement work and proved to her employer that she was even more productive when she was working at home. After the trial period, her employer allowed her to work at home every day. She attends on site meetings once a month. Her daughters are old enough to care for themselves during school holidays. They know that Amy can't be disturbed when she is on the phone, but she is available if they need her.

GETTING DOWN TO BUSINESS

7:00–9:30	Morning routine: breakfast, cleanup, and drives girls to school
10:00–12:00	Work
12:00–1:00	Lunch break
1:00–3:00	Work; Amy's girls ride the bus home from school
3:00–6:00	Errands, homework, activities
6:00–7:00	Dinner
7:00–9:00	Family time
9:00	Girls' bedtime
11:00	Amy's bedtime

Susan

Susan is a married mom with two school-age children. She was an administrative assistant for a large company and was a loyal customer to her friend who sold cosmetics. She decided to join the cosmetics company as a sales representative, but she kept her full-time job. She worked nights and weekends, phoning customers, recruiting other saleswomen, and attending training meetings. She treated her new job as a business right from the beginning. She was meticulous about keeping records, controlled her expenses, and analyzed which marketing methods worked and eliminated those that didn't.

She didn't make a profit immediately, but by carefully controlling her expenses she was able to start earning profits soon after she started. She also was an enthusiastic sales manager for the women who signed up to be part of her sales team. She maintains regular contact with them and helps with any problems they may have. She created her own sales contests, and she joins new team members on their initial sales calls to support them and help improve their presentations.

After building her business for almost a year, she realized that if she devoted herself to cosmetics sales full-time, she would be able to earn a salary close to her full-time income. She loves being there when her children come home from school. They sometimes accompany her when she makes deliveries and they help her fill orders.

Susan continues building her business, and now five years later, she is one of the top saleswomen in her company. She has more than one hundred women working on her team, and through her new website and mailing list, she is adding even more.

Gloria

Gloria is a single mom with four kids, ages six to seventeen. Five years ago, she found herself suddenly single and poor. She hadn't worked outside the home since her oldest daughter was born, but she was determined to stay at home with her children.

She started a home business doing desktop publishing. She produced flyers, newsletters, business cards, and frequent buyer cards for local businesses. Although she cut her household expenses as much as she possibly could, she wasn't earning enough to support her family. Then she met her current employer at a school event. She told him about her business and he mentioned that he worked at home too, designing and selling trade show displays and exhibits for corporations. He also said he could use some sales help, and offered her a commission-based position. Gloria's new boss gave her a list of prospects and when her children were in school, she started making sales calls. She discovered a flare for sales. She loves to talk and meet new people; she followed up with everyone who expressed an interest in her products. She wasn't pushy, but she knew her company offered an excellent product and she was anxious to work with customers to meet their needs. Her new employer was impressed with her results. He had tried working with several other salespeople but no one had achieved results like Gloria.

When she is working on big projects, Gloria's oldest daughter is available to help with her younger siblings, and when Gloria occasionally has to travel, her parents who live nearby, come to stay with the children. She is now making enough money with her business that she could buy a new home for her family. She is an inspiration to everyone she meets.

Barb

Barb was a stay-at-home mom when she started working online. Her website started as a hobby for her. She taught herself how to publish a web page and started posting ideas and advice for other stay-at-home moms. She learned more about creating websites as her site grew and eventually she added message boards, chat rooms, and mailing lists so site visitors could communicate with one another and get to know each other. She recruited other moms she met online to work with her on the site. They moderate discussions and volunteer on different sections of the site such as recipes, crafts, and children's activities. Now her site is one of the most popular online destinations for stay-at-home moms. Barb sells advertising and also uses affiliate programs, which are links she places on her site to other online businesses. When her visitors buy products (books, cosmetics, videos, toys, and clothing) through Barb's links, she receives a percentage of each sale. She is making approximately $1,000 per month through advertising on the site and her affiliate programs.

I Hate Sales

The second thing I hear most often from moms who are looking for a business is, "I don't want to do sales. I hate sales!" I think I understand why.

You all know her, she's a representative for "Happy People Party Plan." We'll call her "Julie." People run the other way when they see her coming. You're her best friend when you're a potential recruit, and you never hear from her again when you say "no." Any gifts you get from Julie are samples of Happy People Party Plan products.

Yet, if you're looking for a home business, the Happy People Party Plan is about the only thing you can find. Can one be successful in the direct sales or network marketing business without becoming like Julie?

When I first started WAHM.com, I had a low opinion of MLM (multi-level marketing) and network marketing in general. In network marketing plans, salespeople are paid not only for the products they sell; they also earn a percentage of the sales from all the people they recruit into the company, their downline. Thus, some network marketers are aggressive recruiters. My experiences with representatives like Julie had left me gun-shy. Plus, I saw a lot of people working very hard at their businesses without really making much money.

DO YOU THINK I'M OVER-DOING IT?

BUY FROM ME!

ASK ME!

HAPPY PEOPLE PARTY PLAN

Perhaps I needed to reexamine my idea of success. Earning just a little extra spending money is not necessarily a bad goal. Not everyone has the energy or desire to make a million dollars, and sometimes paying for gymnastics lessons is enough to break the budget. So that little extra comes in awfully handy. And there are some people who are making decent livings in their network marketing businesses.

Is it possible to be successful in this type of business without sending one's friends and family running for the hills? Can a person who doesn't consider herself "a saleswoman" succeed at sales?

In an effort to create a balanced perspective for myself, I decided to take another look at the direct sales businesses, from the inside. I chose two businesses, one established and one brand new.

The first one sells nutritional products. I realized after I received my start-up kit that this business just wasn't for me. I'm sure many people are successful in this business, but I knew I couldn't get excited about the products or speak enthusiastically about the company. I returned the kit, got my money refunded after a couple phone calls, and that was that. Which is fine. Don't feel that you have to stick with the first business you try. It might just not be the right thing for you, for a variety of reasons. And that's okay.

The second business sells kitchen products. I really like the products, feel that they are reasonably priced, and that they are high quality and useful. The party plan was the only thing that made me hesitate because I'm not a big fan of sales, either. Or at least I didn't think I was. In reality, selling is fun. People give me money, and I give them something they want and/or need. It's great! In the past I've tried to sell things that I was not enthusiastic about. What this made me realize is, it wasn't the *selling* I disliked, it was *not selling*.

Now I still don't consider myself a salesperson, but maybe that will change too. I still have a lot to learn, and I still have all my friends, so . . . so far so good.

Choose Your Products Carefully

When considering what product you will sell, don't just think about the commission plan, focus on the product. Ask yourself, "Is this product something I would want my friends and family to spend their hard-earned money on?" If you can't answer yes to this question, you may have doubts about the value and usefulness of the product. You have to sell with conviction and passion to separate yourself from your competition.

Also, consider the amount of follow-up you may need to do and the cost of the product. If you're selling a $3 product, and need to follow-up with a customer several times to actually achieve a sale, you may make little to no profit. In comparison, if you sell a product for $65, and it's sold on the spot, your profit will be much higher.

Consumable products keep your customers coming back for more. Of course there are many great products that aren't in the consumable category, such as kitchen utensils, toys, and clothes. Many women have success in these businesses. But if you sell a product that lasts forever, your customer will only have to buy that product from you one time. You ensure repeat sales and keep your customers coming back again and again when you sell a product that gets used up.

MONEY MAKING

TIP!

The Plate Is Hot

When you're at a restaurant, and the server tells you "the plate is hot," I'll bet you go ahead and touch the plate anyway. Most people do. Watch them the next time you're out. We get the warning, touch the plate, and then say, "Ouch, that is hot!" Same thing if someone says, "this tastes awful!" We pass the offending food around the table and then we say, "Ewww, that does taste awful!" It seems to be human nature: we have to find out for ourselves.

I see the same phenomenon all the time among people looking for a home business. We've been warned and warned about scams. We either ignore the warnings or we go ahead and fall for the same scams all over again. Why do we have to find out for ourselves? Do we think we're smarter than everyone else is?

Or is it just wishful thinking? The claims sound so good; we really want them to be true. We want to believe that this time, someone will pay us $3 to lick an envelope and Bill Gates really will send us $10,000 for forwarding email. It would be so easy, if only it were true. The women I know who are successful in their home businesses have all achieved their success through a lot of hard work.

Next time you're considering sending money to someone who is making outrageous claims, stop and think. This time won't be different; once a scam, always a scam. Use common sense, and if it sounds too good to be true, it is too good to be true.

Before you get burned, just remember, the plate is hot!

Scam Alert

We've all seen the ads that claim to be hiring home workers. Beware, many of them are scams. Here are some warning signals that will help you weed out the scams from the legitimate jobs.

- They ask for money. They may claim that you need to send money to "show you are serious" or "to cover our costs."
  This is a giant red flag! Don't do it! You should never have to pay someone to work for them. Getting hired to do a job is different from starting a home business. You may have to pay for a starter kit when you begin many direct sales businesses, but they should be very clear about exactly what is in your kit: what you're getting for your money.

- Ads that emphasize WORK AT HOME but are vague about the actual work you will be doing are another danger area. They may say that you will be selling "reports" or typing "orders," but again, they are vague regarding the actual products or services.

- Ads for assemblers: you will have to pay to get your supplies (first red flag), but here's the big catch. In assembly scams, the company has to approve the work you do. They might approve your first or second batches, but after you purchase a large amount of supplies, your work will be rejected because it's "full of flaws," and you will be stuck with your expensive supplies.

- Ads for envelope stuffers: just don't do it. Think about it. Why would anyone pay $2 to $3 to someone simply to put paper in an envelope and apply a stamp? They won't. Most often, after you pay for your supplies, you will be instructed to place ads recruiting others to stuff envelopes. The envelopes you will be stuffing will be the letters you send out trying to sell others on the same scam you just fell for.

- The ads claim that "No experience is necessary" and "Make easy $$$$." Of course there are jobs that offer on-the-job training, but the majority of employers prefer someone with skills and experience. If they lead their ad with these come-ons, watch out. It's another warning signal.

Have you ever been scammed by a work-at-home opportunity?

Yes, I tried a home assembly job. I bought my first kit and received payment for the first product I assembled. But then, after I spent a lot more money for more supplies, they rejected everything else I made.

I fell for a mail order/envelope-stuffing scam. I didn't make a dime. Need I say more?

I paid $25 to start an "email processor" job. What a waste. I just got a list of places to submit ads to advertise for other people to send me money so they could become "email processors."

I paid $70 for a typing-from-home scam. A disk arrived with hundreds of company names and addresses (no phone numbers). Most had restrictive comments like "must be local" or "only accepting applications for overload work" and countless other restrictions. When it came down to it, there were probably only five to ten real possibilities. I sent my application to those and never received any response. The rest of the disk contained common sense "tips" for getting typing at home business. I probably would have done better going through my local Yellow Pages.

I was taken once. I sent money in response to an ad that offered work at home, but asked for $20 up front to prove that I was serious. I never heard from them again after they got my money.

Government Contracts

Every state, county, and city has projects that may be a match for your home business. The first place to look for contracts is on the Internet under your state's name. Your state's website can be found at: www.state.xx.us where "xx" is the two-character abbreviation for your state. For example, the state of California can be found at www.state.ca.us.

At the site, there will be a section labeled "doing business with the state" or "bid opportunities." This area will list the types of contracts currently available in your area. It also lists the categories and specifics of the contracts, such as professional services, printing, consulting, janitorial, management services, legal services, and training. You can also call the contracts office for information, or take a class on how to do business with a government agency.

One thing to keep in mind is that most good contracts, although they may be profitable, are also very demanding. You may be on-call, be required to attend meetings, and you may have to deal with committees and many different individuals. Read the project description carefully so you have a clear understanding of what will be expected.

Another option is sub-contracting for another business. Many companies that win government contracts sub-contract for a portion of the work. They may need people to do typesetting, word processing, database design, or any of the numerous tasks associated with a given project. They may be open to having their sub-contractors work from their own home offices. Sub-contracting positions are often advertised in the classified ads of your local newspaper.

TIP!

But Where Are the Giraffes?

As my daughter's fifth birthday approached, we were trying to decide what to do for her birthday party. There were so many decisions to be made. It was a big birthday for a little girl, so I told her that she could choose where to have her party. I presented her options: Chuck E. Cheese, McDonald's, The Gym, a pool party, or a pizza party. She finally decided on a zoo party. Our local zoo has a great birthday program. A zookeeper brings a few animals to your home, talks about them, and gives the children a chance to pet or hold the animal. They might bring a ferret, a snake, or an owl. So great, she decided on the zoo party. I waited a couple days just to be sure she wouldn't change her mind. Then, as I was about to send the deposit to the zoo, I asked one last time, "Now, you're sure you want the zoo party?"

"Yes," she said, "I think my friends will like it, and we've never had giraffes at our house before."

Back to the drawing board.

I think choosing a business can be such a difficult decision because there are just too many choices. I often get letters from women who really want to work from home, but they don't know what to do. I think to myself, "How can that be? There are so many things to choose from, so many businesses that can be run from home."

Perhaps that is the problem. Too many choices.

So how does one decide what to do, how do you pick your party? I always tell people to think about the things that they like to do, their skills and interests, and try to build a business around that. And look at the businesses other women are running, borrow ideas from them. If you choose something you enjoy, you will have a better chance of success. But be careful that you have realistic expectations; we're "work" at home moms for a good reason. If someone is trying to sell you on a business, they are going to present their best possible story, and tell you why their company is best.

It is up to you to ask the questions, find out exactly what is expected and what kind of results the typical person can expect. Find out exactly what animals they will bring to the party, and then make your decision.

My daughter still had her zoo birthday, because animals were her "thing" at the time, and she had a great time. I just needed to make sure that she had realistic expectations.

Of course, as difficult as it is, choosing the business is the easy part. As every birthday mom knows, once the "party" starts, then the real work begins . . . running your business.

Just watch out for the giraffes.

wahm.com

MONEY MAKING

TIP!

Getting Online

If you've been avoiding getting on the Internet because you feel intimidated by computers, it's time to get off the sidelines. It's not nearly as difficult as you might imagine. America Online is a good service for beginners. You can also find helpful information in beginner books such as *The Internet for Dummies*, by John Levine, IDG books Worldwide, 2000.

If you already have a computer and modem, you're halfway there. If you're shopping for a computer, choose your computer based on the way it will be used. Most of us don't need the most recent, fastest processors. A good middle-of-the-road machine with a high-speed modem will fill the needs of most home businesses.

Choosing an Internet Service Provider (ISP)

Most national services offer unlimited time plans for about $20 per month, and many of these services are now included with the purchase of a PC. AOL, Prodigy, and MSN are examples of national services that are easy to use and most also offer free server space to host your own website.

You can start using these services by picking up a free CD-ROM you will find in magazines and on newsstands. The CD-ROMs contain the software and information you need to get started. Local service providers are an alternative to the big national services. Find them in your phone book or in the ads in free computer newspapers that are available in most communities. Local service providers may offer more personalized assistance to get you started, and if you are in a rural community, they may offer service where the national providers don't. Be careful that your provider's access phone numbers are local calls for you so you don't have to pay long-distance phone charges when you're online.

Email

One of the beauties of email is that you can communicate with people at any time of the day, or night. You can reach people all over the world for no more than the cost of a local phone call, and your clients will never know that your toddler was singing the *Barney* theme song at the top of his lungs while you were writing the email. Auto-responders are another helpful email feature. An auto-responder is kind of like a pre-recorded message you can send to people who request information from you. For example, if you have a link on your website that says, "send me more information" your auto-responder will automatically send an email to anyone who clicks on the link or writes to your auto-responder email address. The email can contain all of your business or product information, or anything else you wish, because you have pre programmed it. You write the email once, but it gets sent out again and again. What a timesaver!

MONEY MAKING

Mailing Lists

Also called Listservs, or email loops, they are populated by people who share a common interest. There are lists for work-at-home moms, stay-at-home moms, moms who are writers, moms who have website design business. You name it, there is a probably a list for you. Some of these lists are very high traffic, and you can expect to get many emails every day. In this case, check to see if there is a digest option. When you subscribe to a digest version, you will receive the daily emails in a single email, usually with a file attached, which contains all of the emails in one "digest."

When you first subscribe to a list, carefully read the rules of the list so you know what and what is not allowed. Then "lurk" for awhile to get a feeling for the conversations on the list. Most lists frown on blatant advertising of your business, but you can almost always offer helpful advice to other list members and add your "signature" which can include your business information and website address.

TIP!

Chat

I network with many other women who publish websites. We communicate mainly through email, but occasionally it's nice to "talk" to one another in real-time too. Chat rooms have gotten a bad reputation in the media, but they're not all bad. If you have business associates with whom you would like to meet, you can arrange to meet in one of the many private chat rooms online. That way you know who is in the chat room with you and you can all easily communicate with one another.

MONEY
MAKING

TIP!

Message Boards

Most large websites also offer message boards for a variety of interests. Again, most of these frown on blatant ads, but you can usually include your business information in your signature. Be sure to read the rules before you post on any message board.

Websites

A website is probably one of the biggest money-saving devices you can employ for your business. You can create a multi-page, full-color, online "brochure" that can be viewed by anyone at any time, and it really isn't difficult to do. Your ISP may provide space for your website, and there are other sites that offer free space such as Geocities and Tripod (www.geocities.com, and www.tripod.com).

In exchange for the free server space, these sites display ads on your pages. They also make it easy for you to build your site by walking you through the process. You can have your own site online in an amazingly short time.

Other sites host websites for fees starting at about $20 per month. You will want to use them if you want more control over your pages, or if you want to own your own domain name (www.mybusiness.com), and you can use an HTML (hypertext markup language) editor to create your own files. There are text editors that require you to learn HTML and there are WYSI-WYG (what you see is what you get) editors that let you point-and-click to create your pages. They are about as easy to use as a word processing program. Once you have your files, you need to upload them to your server space. Your Internet service provider can usually help you with this step and also help you register your domain name. The cost to register your domain is $35 per year, plus any setup fees your Internet service provider charges, usually ranging from $0 to $50.

Affiliate Programs

Another way to make money from your website is through affiliate programs. The first affiliate programs were for books and they are still popular. Now however, you can also place links on your site to many products and services and receive a commission on all sales that result from your links. Link Share (www.linkshare.com) is an example of a company that helps you manage all of your affiliate programs.

Online Resources

Some of the best resources and advice for home business owners can be found online, and most of them are available to you for no charge. WAHM.com lists links to the best websites for your business and family at www.wahm.com/links.html.

Checklist: approximate costs of getting your business online

Computer, monitor and printer	$500 to $3000
Website design software	$50
Monthly internet access	$20
Website hosting	$20 per month
Domain registration onetime	$35 per year plus setup fee: $0 to $50

MY COMPUTER CRASHES SO OFTEN I'M THINKING ABOUT INSTALLING AIR BAGS

TIP!

CHAPTER FOUR

Making the Transition

Now you've chosen your business, but even if you've prepared yourself and given this a lot of thought, you will probably need some time to adjust to your new lifestyle. Working at home may be a major change in the structure of your family. Don't assume that everything will be perfect right from the start.

Adding a New Member to the Family

Starting a home business is like adding another member to your family. As you can imagine, this will require some adjustment on everyone's part. Your priorities and expectations will determine how well you all adjust; communication, help, and humor will make the transition easier.

First of All, Determine Your Priorities

Defining what you expect from your business and family is important before you start your business. What are your priorities? Do you need to have a clean house? Make lots of money? Have free time for yourself? Will your spouse be supportive? Will your children be expected to help with the business or will the business be off-limits to them?

Will you work regular hours?

For me, one of my top priorities is my family, which is why I chose a home business in the first place. When all is said and done, I would rather say I've had a marginally successful business and a successful family life than having enjoyed a phenomenally successful business career and only a marginally successful family life.

Besides, God willing, I'll have many, many years to work after my children are grown. And I do believe that it's possible to combine business and family successfully. When I first started my business, I went back to a list of priorities I had written as a college assignment. I sat down and listed all the things that were important to me. They fell under such categories as family, health, business, religion, money, fun and recreation, security, and recognition.

I then numbered them to determine my priorities. I'm amazed and somewhat embarrassed when I look back on the first list I wrote while I was still in college. Aging has changed me quite a bit, thank goodness. I won't share the entire list with you, but I will say that fun and recreation ranked much higher 15 years ago than they do now. Doing this exercise may make you think about things a little differently, and it will help you clarify your priorities.

Adjust Your Expectations

Notice I didn't say lower your expectations. Having worked in software, I've acquired the ability to turn a bug into a feature. If a computer doesn't work exactly as anticipated, a good software engineer will find a way to turn that into a feature of the program: "The date reads January 1, 1900? Right, we meant to do that. It gives us the feeling of going back to a more relaxed time."

You can look at household tasks in the same way. As Joan Rivers said, "I don't clean my bathtub anymore. When I have company, I just take a marker and label the bathtub ring, 'Fill to Here.'" Now that's turning what most people would see as a problem into a feature.

If my house were ever burglarized, the crooks would just turn around and leave without taking anything. They would think someone had beaten them to the job. My house is pre-ransacked! That's a feature. You may not be comfortable letting things slide quite that much; however, you'd be well advised to find your own comfort level and relax a little.

Most moms find that the first days running our home businesses are like a honeymoon. We are filled with enthusiasm and excitement. We have planned and pre-pared and feel like nothing can stand in our way. I'll never forget the feeling I had when I got my first home business contract. I walked with my head held higher. I felt like putting a sign around my neck, "I am a business woman!"

Then reality sets in, and reality doesn't always meet our expectations. The jobs might not come along regu-larly. The day-to-day challenges of running a business start to take their toll. A lot of moms give up at this stage. Adjust your expectations and realize that this is normal and to be expected. Take advantage of local networking groups and support groups. Talk to other moms at home, other moms who are working at home if you can. They will understand what you're going through, and often just talking to someone else who understands can help you get through the tough times. Also keep your priori-ties clear, go back to your priority list. Remind yourself why you started the business in the first place, and keep your focus on your long-term goals.

Communicate

Don't expect your spouse and children to be psychic. If you require something of them, let them know. Now that you've established your priorities and expectations, communicate them to your family. And be specific. I get more help if I say to my husband, "Please empty the dishwasher and make eggs and toast for the girls" than if I just ask, "Will you help in the kitchen?"

My children know that when the business line rings, they need to be quiet. It's like a drill now. Whenever my business phone rings, they'll say "business line" and then settle down. I don't always choose to answer if we're in the middle of something—I let it go to voice mail. But if I'm expecting a call, they know the drill.

I also tell my family the details of my business problems or successes, and sometimes discuss questions I have with them. We are always talking. We make a point of sitting down for meals together so we can all share what is happening in our lives. We usually keep the radio off in the car and use this time for talking, too. We set goals together and choose something fun that we will all do with the business money when our goal is reached. It can be as simple as a night out for ice cream or as big as a family vacation. This way, they also reap the rewards of the business. And I often get great ideas from my husband and my daughters. When we were discussing the marketing plan for this book, my five-year-old suggested putting "This is NOT Cheryl's book" on all of the other books at the bookstore. Maybe not the most practical suggestion, but not a bad idea.

Accept Help

Since time is a limited resource, you'll want to spend it in the most efficient manner possible. If you're billing work out at the rate of $40 an hour and can hire someone to do house cleaning or yard work for $10 an hour, do it. (And then send me their number.) No one will think less of you if you don't clean your own toilets.

Face the fact that you can't do everything. Get out your priority list again. If you don't want to turn over full-time care of your children to someone else, explore other options. Maybe have a sitter come into your home occasionally or share part-time child care with another home-based parent. Then plan your client meetings and work during those hours. Hire a neighborhood teenager to help out with chores around the house. Subcontract with other moms to handle some business tasks. Hire someone to do your bookkeeping or pay a commission for sales help.

Help is out there; accept it.

Keep Your Sense of Humor

I think this is most important. There are always two ways to look at a situation. You and only you have control over your attitude and how you'll react to a given situation.

When my husband helps out around the house, I have to remember that he will have a different style of doing things than I do. For example, one time he made a tuna fish and bologna sandwich for my daughter. Yes, you read that right—tuna and bologna.

I could have gotten angry or I could have laughed. I chose to laugh. In fact, we're still laughing about it. You see, I had been making tuna fish salad for my daughter and she saw me putting in the Miracle Whip and asked what I was doing. I said, "making tuna fish." So, in her mind, Miracle Whip was tuna fish.

A few days later, I was working. I had a deadline looming, my husband was watching the kids, and I asked him to please, please keep them occupied. I really couldn't be disturbed.

He was making bologna sandwiches for lunch. (Do you get the impression we're not health food nuts?) Thinking back to the Miracle Whip, our

UH... DAD? THIS IS NOT HOW MOM MAKES A TUNA FISH SANDWICH!

daughter asked him to put tuna fish on her bologna sandwich. Not wanting to make waves, he did as asked. Of course, she freaked out when he served her the strange concoction.

I came in to see what was causing all the commotion, which was what he was trying to avoid in the first place. Imagine my surprise to see my frustrated husband, my screaming daughter, and a bologna and tuna fish sandwich on the table. Sometimes you just have to laugh.

Choosing the Structure for Your Business

You have several choices when designing the structure of your business.

- **Sole Proprietorship**
  This is the least expensive and least complicated. You and your business are viewed as the same, and you will be personally liable for any losses your business incurs. Regulations vary from state to state, but if you are doing business in a name other then your own, you will most likely need to register as a DBA (Doing Business As).

- **Corporation**
  The main advantage you get when you incorporate is some protection from personal liability. Your corporation is separate from you as an individual. It also can make your business seem more substantial; there is status that comes with the CEO title. You will have your board of directors to advise you and help you grow your business. However, it is more complicated and expensive to establish and maintain than a sole proprietorship or a partnership.

- **Profit or Nonprofit**
  If you choose to incorporate as a nonprofit, it doesn't mean that you can't make any money. The corporate directors can still be paid a salary. However, the rules are very complicated and you definitely need legal advice from an attorney familiar with nonprofit incorporation if you are thinking about going the nonprofit route. Religious, charitable, and educational companies are examples of some businesses that may qualify for nonprofit status.

- **Partnership**
  If you are working on your business with a friend, you are usually considered partners whether or not you have filed a formal partnership agreement. Working in a partnership gives you someone with whom you can share your business expenses and burdens, and you can combine your resources to build the business. But you will also be personally responsible for your partner's business liabilities, and no matter how well you are getting along now,

you may have serious disagreements. Partnerships almost always start happily; formal agreements make for happy endings too.

You may change the structure of your business as your business grows and your needs change. For example, you may wish to start as a sole proprietor and incorporate at a later date. It is essential that you consult with your attorney and accountant to determine which structure is best for you.

wahm.com

GETTING DOWN TO BUSINESS

Your Business Plan

Many WAHMs are tempted to skip this step, but it will really help you clarify your strategy and goals. Unless you're seeking financing, your business plan doesn't have to be long and formal. Consider these areas as you prepare your plan.

- **What is your business?**

What products will you sell or what service will you provide? In this section, describe in detail your product or service and your vision for your business.

- **Who will buy this product or service?**

Think about your potential customers. Why do people need what you have to offer? How and when will you be able to sell your service or product? Will you meet your customers face-to-face? Will you sell your products online?

- **Who is your competition?**

Look at other businesses. Is there anyone else providing your product or service? What will you do differently? Why will people buy from you instead of your competitors? Will you be able to use your status as a work-at-home mom to your advantage to market to other moms or people who support your lifestyle?

- **Financials**

What will your costs be? Examine all of your expenses, start-up costs, marketing costs, and ongoing costs. How much will you charge? Is there real profit potential?

- **Marketing**

How will people find out about your business? How will you promote the business and find new customers? Keep the 4 P's in mind: Product, Placement, Promotion, and Price. What product are you selling? From where will you sell it? Mail order, direct sales, boutiques? How much will you spend promoting it? At what price will you sell it?

- **Management**

This section is unique to work-at-home moms. How will you manage your home and business? Think about how you will integrate your business with your family's schedule. How will you handle sick days? Will you travel for your business? Do you have a support system established that can help you when you have deadlines or sick children? Will your business be flexible enough that you can work around your family's schedule?

For extra help, the Small Business Administration offers free online classes on their website: http://classroom.sba.gov.

wahm.com

GETTING DOWN TO BUSINESS

Ode to an Office Chair

My rear end is speaking to me this morning. No, this doesn't happen often, but when it does, it's hard to ignore.

"Buy a decent office chair!" It cries.

I've been sitting here at my keyboard, sitting on the only expendable chair in the house, the only chair I was able to take without anyone noticing it's missing. Sitting here since 3 a.m. and my rear can't take it anymore.

My children and husband covet any furniture I try to claim as my own. Any decent chair is returned to its place of origin, as quickly as they can wrestle it away from me. So I end up (no pun intended) with this old wooden rocker.

This old armless rocker that is too uncomfortable to be used in any other room in the house. This old rocker in which my mom rocked me to sleep. Its edges rubbed smooth from years of use. I rocked my girls in this old chair too. Plenty of sleepless nights were spent in this chair. Sick babies and worried moms, peaceful babies and content moms. Moms who loved their children, rocked them, and passed that love on to them. I hope there will be many more moms and babies rocking in this chair, long after my sore butt and I are long gone.

So yes, I should get a new office chair, not because my back and behind deserve it, but because this old chair deserves it. It deserves to be cared for and it deserves to be passed on to the next generation of mothers and babies, so someday those mothers can say,

"Your great-grandma and your grandma rocked their babies in this chair—just like I'm rocking you."

Setting Up Your Home Office

Depending on the business you choose you may have to buy a little or a lot of office equipment to get started. You can make your home office environment as personal as you wish, and you will want to make it flexible. Home business owners are often given the advice to completely separate their work and home spaces. However, this advice doesn't always work for work-at-home moms. I hear from many moms who started out assuming that they want their office set up in an isolated part of the house, only to find out later that they would rather have their computer in the center of the household activity. Time will tell what works best for you.

Many business owners are tempted to over spend in this phase. They want the latest technology, the most modern office furniture, the best business stationery, and the nicest business cards. Be careful that you don't spend all your profits before you earn them. Two small filing cabinets with a board placed over them can be a functional desk. Of course you will probably need to buy some supplies: pens, bulletin board, maybe a cordless phone; just don't go overboard. Figure out the minimum that you need to spend to get started, and budget for the things you would like to add as you start making a profit.

Your accountant can help you figure out what supplies you can write off on your taxes and what is the best way to structure your office space in regards to the home office tax deduction. It is a good idea to consult with him or her before you make any major home office purchases.

Many work-at-home moms also set up an office space for their children. Check second hand and consignment shops for used desks, easels, and even an old-fashioned typewriter. Children often like working alongside mom, and it helps establish good organizational habits for them, too.

Your car can serve as your field office. You can carry product samples and paperwork; when you find yourself waiting to pick up your children from school or sports practices, you can use the time to your advantage. If you organize it carefully, you can work quite efficiently from your car. Many WAHMs use different color plastic bins or baskets to keep their supplies and paperwork

wahm.com

GETTING DOWN TO BUSINESS

organized in their cars. We also like the seat back organizers for children that attach to the back of the front seats that hold markers, pencils, papers, and games.

A WAHM I know who sells children's books always has a supply of books in her trunk. The parents at her children's school look for her when they need to buy a birthday gift or just want to see her new products. Because she's organized and always has products with her, she makes many sales from the trunk of her car. You can buy magnetic signs or vinyl letters that attach to your car, so you can advertise your business whenever you're on the road. You can also use your car time to listen to motivational and/or educational audiotapes. Your car can become an extension of your home office.

When you work at home, you have the power to choose your work environment. You can make it as traditional or unique as you wish. Because, above all, it's your business!

Do you have a separate space for your office?

I do have a separate office for my business. It is pretty essential that I do, since I'm manufacturing and the equipment and supplies I use take up a lot of space and can be dangerous around the kids. It's extremely messy, too.

I don't have a home office, but I do have a corner. We've got the computer set up in the dining room, and I try to keep my papers in some kind of order in a file briefcase. We realize that we need to make some changes that will give me privacy from the TV and the kids if I'm really going to make this work. I'm hopeful.

I actually have three offices. I have a wonderful home office (fax machine, computer, separate phone) in the downstairs part of the house. However, it is too far from the everyday flow of the household, so I usually work in my second and third "offices," the kitchen table and the living room computer area. Of course I have to fight for this space whenever I have to work because the family believes it is their space. But I wouldn't exchange any of it for a high-rise view. Where else would I be allowed to hang finger-painted pictures on the walls?

Note from Cheryl: The previous two responses are good examples of the different needs of different moms and families. The first mom has discovered that she needs more peace and quiet to be able to work productively, while mom #2 has found just the opposite. For her to be productive, she needs to be in the middle of the traffic flow of her house.

The den is set up as a work area for me and a play area for the kids. I also have a notebook computer that migrates to the bedroom for the early morning hours before the kids are up and when they are sleeping, or to the living room so the older one can play in the yard under my view.

I am a visiting nurse and I work out of my car and end up doing a lot of paperwork on the living room floor. The computer takes up any desk space I might have for a home office.

I share my "deluxe" office with the family washer, dryer, and cat box.

TIME
SAVING

TIP!

Great Gadgets for WAHMs

There are many gadgets that make our work-at-home lives easier. Here are a few that you can use to help you work more efficiently.

- **Cellular phones** are great time savers. You can make calls while you're waiting to pick up your children at school, or out at the park. A note of caution, however: driving requires all of your attention. No call is so important that it can't wait until you stop the car. So use your cell phone when you're away from home but don't take any safety risks for the sake of a few minutes on the phone.

- **Wireless headset.** If you spend a lot of time on the phone when you're working at home, consider buying a wireless hands-free headset. You will free your hands to do other chores, typing, or even doing the dishes. You will also free yourself from neck strain caused by cradling the phone between your ear and shoulder.

- **Voice mail** has the advantage over a standard answering machine because callers can leave messages if your line is busy. If you have only one phone line and you're online a lot, use voice mail and your customers will never get a busy signal.

- **Caller ID** helps you determine which calls should be answered right away and which can go to voice mail. Combine caller ID with a wireless phone and you have even more freedom.

- **Personal digital assistants** or **PDAs** are powerful little computers. You can keep track of your schedule, address book, check your email, and take notes. Think of it as an organizer that fits in the palm of your hand.

- **Digital voice recorder.** If you find you get your best ideas at the most inopportune moments, a digital voice recorder will come in handy. Many recorders also come with software that can learn your voice patterns. When the recorder is connected to your computer it converts your speech to text.

CHAPTER FIVE

Taking Care of Your Home While Running Your Home Business

Remember that as a work-at-home mom, your home becomes part of your business. You work where you live and live where you work. I was surprised when I first started working at home to find that my home was never really used before, when I was working away from home. Now I have to manage my home—and my home business.

Find your comfort level and realize that you're not alone. We're all struggling to find the right balance.

Your Home and Your Business

When you work at home, you may find that you care more about your home environment. You don't walk out the door in the morning and come back again at night. Now you are at home all day, and your home is really getting used. But because you're still working, you don't necessarily have more time to devote to housekeeping.

Being a work-at-home mom can also bring up some housekeeping situations that most business people don't have to deal with.

I know a work-at-home mom who was perplexed

by a large smudge on all the charge card receipts she ran through her machine, until she discovered a raisin that was squished inside the machine. Another mom was meeting with a client at her home when she discovered that she had sat on her child's chocolate bar that had been left on her office chair.

Don't feel that you have to live up to someone else's expectations. You and your family need to work together to find the housekeeping level that works best for you. How much disarray can you live with? Some families insist on keeping just one area of their home spotless. That way they always have a place where they can entertain guests if someone stops by, without having to clear away clutter. Many moms let things slide during the week and clean like crazy on Saturday morning. Other families do a little each day and have specific daily jobs assigned to each family member.

Talk with your family, work together, decide what will work best for all of you, and keep everyone happy.

Housekeeping and Children

Housekeeping tasks can take over all of your free time. But you can actually minimize the time you spend taking care of day-to-day chores by working with your children and following these simple steps:

- Teach your children to clean up after themselves. Keep small brooms and dust pans, a Dustbuster, and paper towels where they can reach them when they need to clean up a small spill.

- If your children tend to be competitive, make up cleaning contests. Try the bed-making dash or the take-out-the trash triathlon. Use a stopwatch; create charts of personal bests and household record holders. Blue ribbons and trophies can be purchased inexpensively at discount stores or party supply stores and they really add to the fun.

- Limit your cleaning time and set a timer. Designate your cleaning time into 10-minute intervals during which everybody pitches in to clean the house. You'll be surprised at how much you can accomplish in a short time if everyone focuses on his or her tasks. Since there's a time limit, helpers are less likely to drag their feet.

- A trip through the car wash is a big treat for my kids. Get your children to help vacuum, wash the windows, and clean the inside of the car with the payoff being a trip through the wash.

TIME SAVING TIP!

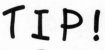

I'm a Housewife?

When I made the decision to leave the traditional workplace to stay home and take care of my girls, I didn't feel any different, and I didn't expect that anyone would treat me differently. I was wrong. In fact, the first time someone called me a housewife, I had a major identity crisis.

My insurance agent was filling out paperwork: Name? Address? Occupation? Occupation . . . I wasn't sure how to answer that one, being new to the stay-at-home business. "I . . . I'm . . . I guess I'm a mom." I answered. I watched him write in the occupation line: "Housewife."

NOW **THIS** IS THE BEST PERFORMANCE REVIEW I'VE EVER RECEIVED !

WORLD'S GREATEST MOM !

I couldn't believe it! How could I, one who has never considered the relative merits of different brands of fabric softener, be labeled a housewife? June Cleaver was a housewife, but me? I didn't think so.

I complained to my husband that night, "All my life, I've been something. A student, an engineer, but what am I now?"

I didn't realize my daughter had been listening, she piped in with her answer, "You're a MOM!" She said, just as I answered, "What am I now? Nothing!"

She was so proud to have figured out the answer and the look on her face when she heard me say "nothing" broke my heart. She was right, I'm a mom above all else. I've never felt like a "nothing" since that moment.

As you make the transition from working mom to work-at-home mom, I think you, too, will find that "mom" is the best job description you've ever had.

Seven Habits of Happy WAHMs

I was listening to a time-management expert on a talk show the other day. He was asked how families can find more time to spend with one another. One of his recommendations was to hire someone to do your laundry. Hire someone to do my laundry? Even if I assumed I had the money to pay someone to do the laundry, I'm not sure I would want a stranger going through our dirty laundry. My dirty dishes, yes. My laundry? I don't think so. Besides, doing the laundry in our house doesn't really consume that much time anyway. Now, we do occasionally pay for our haste with a few pink socks, but that's a small price to pay for quick laundry service. If you're combining a home business with all the other jobs of raising kids and running a home, something has to give.

Personally, I need solutions that are more practical than, "hire someone to do it." I have learned a few helpful things these past few years, from books, personal experience and trial and error. Here are my seven habits for happy WAHMs:

1. Clean your clothes when you clean yourself. Keep your hand-washable hamper in the bathroom. Then when you hop in the shower or tub, grab a sweater or slip, and kill two birds with one stone. That way you can spend the afternoon taking a bubble bath and complain to your husband that you spent all afternoon doing the laundry.

2. A place for everything and everything in its place. Think like a kindergarten teacher and create little cubbies and containers for everything. Give everything a "home" and cleanup becomes much easier, and it can even be fun. It used to drive me crazy that my daughter was the most helpful little cleaner at school, at the store, everywhere but home. Then it dawned on me, it's fun to clean up when it's clear where things belong.

3. Shirt's wrinkled? Throw it in the dryer with a damp towel, walk away, and return a few minutes later to a wrinkle-free shirt. Who needs to iron?

4. Strap sponges on the kids' feet and turn them loose in the kitchen.

5. Little kids love to do dishes; let them. Sure they splash around a bit, who cares? Just don't give them anything sharp or breakable. That leaves plastic dishes, which are considered our "fine china" anyway.

6. Keep Barbie barefoot. Don't even try to keep track of her shoes. As soon as my girls get a new Barbie, we have her say, "My feet are killing me! Get me out of these shoes!" Barbie's much happier and so am I.

7. Finally, and most importantly, when the dishes and laundry and toys are stacked up and you think you can't take it anymore, give your kids a hug, and don't worry about it! Because one day, you will look around and the laundry and dirty dishes will still be there, but your kids won't be. They will grow up and move on with their lives. Now if I could just come up with a way to send those Barbie shoes with them . . .

Scheduled Cleaning

Remember the June Cleaver days? Monday was laundry day, Tuesday ironing. Even in our modern age, designating specific days for individual chores can do a lot to simplify your life. Take care of laundry one day, bathrooms another; floors, windows, grocery shopping, all get their own day. By limiting these tasks to separate days you won't get overwhelmed feeling like you have to do everything, every day.

One caveat: don't let your schedule rule you. Before you get into too much of a rut, throw a curve into your schedule and be spontaneous. Skip laundry day and go on a picnic, or take a trip to the bookstore.

Just don't do it too often or you'll be back to doing everything every day.

The Boomerang Books

When working at home, keeping your home neat and organized can be a huge challenge. It is a constant struggle for me, and I'm always looking for a secret or system that will work for us.

So this past weekend I started reading one of my many organizing books: *Ten Simple Steps to an Organized Life*. These books, as it turns out, are much like diet books. Just reading the book does absolutely nothing to solve the problem. So, I sent my family out for a few hours and decided to tackle step #1: Clean out your bookshelves.

That didn't sound too difficult. I grabbed a couple of empty boxes and started weeding out the books that we could donate or throw away. Two hours later, I had lots of empty shelf space and two big boxes of old books.

But then my family came back home. My oldest daughter, Nicki, went right for the boxes. "What are you doing?" she asked.

"I'm going to give these books away. It will help clear out the clutter, and we never read these books anymore anyway."

She picked up *Pat the Possum*. "Mom! This was my favorite book when I was little! How could you throw this away?" She put it back on the shelf, and proceeded to replace all of her early readers that she claimed she simply couldn't part with.

My youngest daughter, Dani, sensed the urgency and joined her sister's crusade. "What is this book called?" She asked.

Learn to Speak Greek

"Mom! I've always wanted to do that!" Fine, back on the shelf it went.

But I didn't give up, I protested, "Please kids, we have to clear out some of the junk in this house."

"Well how about all of these books then?" Nicki pointed to the top shelf.

"My Oprah Book Collection? Are you crazy? I couldn't possibly part with those."

My husband even pitched in. "Hey, *Football Through the Ages*, I've been looking for that!" Back on the shelf.

I couldn't take it anymore. I left the room, and returned to find the shelves once again loaded with books, and my two boxes empty. Except for one book, there on the bottom of the box: *Ten Simple Steps to an Organized Life.*

wahm.com

GETTING
DOWN TO
BUSINESS

Consulting

Are you an expert in something? Would you like to make money with your knowledge? You may want to consider a consulting home business. There are women running successful consulting businesses on subjects ranging from computers to gardening—everything in between. I know of a work-at-home mom who started a successful magazine, sold it, and now advises clients starting their own magazines. Another mom, a computer consultant, specializes in teaching senior citizens about the Internet. Do you have a flair for organizing? Consult on organizing homes. Are you a cleaning whiz? Teach other moms how to make their housekeeping more efficient.

As with any home business, you need to create a business plan and evaluate your market. Will your customers be individuals or large companies? Will you charge by the hour or by the project? Draw up a formal contract to present to your clients so they know exactly what services you will provide and what your fees are.

If Housework Brings One Closer to God, I'm in Heaven

I have a friend who reads houses. She claims that she can tell the state of a couple's marriage, their financial status—in fact, everything about them—just by observing their home. She checks out the housekeeping, decorating, bookshelves. From these, she finds out all she needs to know to size up their domestic situation.

I'm afraid to ask her what my house says to her.

It seems no matter how hard I try to keep up, toys, mail, and newspapers creep out of their hiding places and invade my house. I swear the neighbors bring over dirty dishes while we sleep.

And since my "free time" is spent working on my business, the day-to-day chores slide . . . just a little.

I take comfort in something I read a long time ago: The more intelligent one is, the more cluttered their living environment. I don't know if it's true or not—if it is—I'm a genius!

Even I have my limits, though. A recent news report about a house fire told a sad story, but the worst thing I heard was, "The firefighters were hampered by the large amount of debris in the house."

Can you imagine? I honestly think that even worse than losing my home and possessions (if no one was hurt, of course) would be having our local news anchor tell the entire city that my house was a mess!

How humiliating.

So, we all pitch in, everyone does their share, and we manage to keep the debris just below the level where it becomes a news item.

Rules for a WAHM Home

Our local teachers came pretty close to going out on strike here last week, which got me thinking. Since I have a home business, what can I do when things aren't going my way? What about the times I need more help, better working conditions, or more money? Going out on strike isn't an option for me. If I'm not here working, nothing will get done. It's even hard for me to take a sick day.

And there are days, not too many, but there are those days when I have to wonder if this is all worth it. I recently got an email from a WAHM wannabe. She said, "You're living my dream." I looked around and thought, "Then I'd hate to see your nightmare!"

THE PILE OF DIRTY DISHES IN MY SINK IS ONE OF THE FEW MANMADE OBJECTS THAT CAN BE SEEN FROM SPACE

We do occasionally get caught up on housekeeping, but then things slowly start to slide again. We had company last week and one of the girls reached under a sofa cushion and pulled out . . . a can of Cheez Whiz! Of course she couldn't discreetly hand it to me; it had to be announced and displayed for all to see. I guess it was funny, and it could have been worse. Heaven knows what's living under those cushions.

So I made the decision that I need to post a list of rules for visitors:

1. Don't lift any sofa or chair cushions, and for heaven's sake NEVER reach under one without looking.

2. If a door is closed, it's closed for a reason. DO NOT open it.

3. Don't peek behind the shower curtain. It's not pretty and I won't be responsible for post-traumatic stress syndrome.

4. Don't open closet doors; they are spring loaded. Flying debris may injure you and the doors cannot be shut again without the help of at least three additional people.

5. Don't venture into the laundry room. The last guest that did has never been seen again. We sent out a search party, but they had to give up after three days.

I hope these rules will save me from some embarrassing moments and protect my guests from injuries. I know everything will get taken care of eventually. For the most part, I love working from home, and I'm willing to accept working conditions that some people might consider less than ideal. I won't be going out on strike anytime soon. I'll keep working, and eventually I'll be making enough money with my business so that I can hire the help that I need. Until then . . . pass the Cheez Whiz!

How do you handle housekeeping?

I take advantage of the new products on the market to make cleaning easier. My kids are old enough to help with housework (ages six and nine). On a daily basis one of the girls will go through the house with one of the new dusting cloths and quickly dust, while my other child uses a cloth on the kitchen and bathroom floors. I will give both bathrooms a quick scrub down with the new disinfectant wipes every day or two. We all help clear off the table after dinner and dishes go right into the dishwasher. Every night after dinner, I use a disinfectant spray cleaner so the kitchen is always nice and clean. My kids also need to put their toys and clothes away every night before they go to bed. My husband does the laundry (and he's actually better at it than I am!), and we both usually fold it in our bedroom at night while watching TV. What's left is done on a weekly basis on the weekends and takes me maybe half an hour. I find just keeping on top of the cleaning is a big help because it cuts down on the weekly deep-cleaning we have to do.

How do I handle housework? I pay for it. I am fortunate enough that I live in a small town and house cleaning is not real expensive. If I had to do all of my own housekeeping I could not do anything else. My husband does not do A THING to help because he is never here and I am by myself with my kids all the time. If I had to work just to pay a housekeeper I would do that. My priorities go like this: God, family, work, then the housework—so that gets paid for.

I am one of the fortunate ones whose husband LOVES housework. I do the laundry most of the time, usually at least a load a day. But the rest I leave for him to do on his days off.

Note from Cheryl: Does he have any brothers?

What I did was prioritize by percentages. First I made a list of all my duties by weight of importance. I attributed a certain percentage to each category: God, hubby, me, kids home business work, and housework. Then I calculated the number of hours I'm awake and determined how many hours to spend on each priority. This doesn't have to be rigid or followed no matter what; it's just a plan that assures me that I am sticking to my priorities.

When I Get Around to it

I had been working on a big project for weeks, and was so frustrated with my lack of progress. The weekend arrived and I thought if I could just get some time alone, I would be able to get a lot more done.

So I asked my husband if he could take the girls for a few hours. He agreed to take them out for pizza. The girls were excited for their "Daddy Date" and happily waved goodbye. I stood at the door for a minute, listening to, and enjoying, the silence. Then I headed for the computer . . . well not quite yet; first I better put away those dishes, and I might as well throw in a load of laundry.

On my way to the laundry room, I walked by the mirror and noticed that my eyebrows really needed a good plucking. How long has it been since I've had time to do that? And my toes! Wouldn't a nice coat of fresh polish be just the thing for summer?

Now, back to the laundry . . . then I saw my daughter's dress that needed mending, which would just take a second. After all, if I don't get it fixed soon, she will have outgrown it. Then, throw in another load of laundry, and . . . I'd better iron that shirt for tomorrow.

What a great feeling : . . I was getting so much accomplished.

Then, finally, I sat down at the computer and got ready to really get some work done!

That's when I heard the key in the door . . . "Mom, we're home!"

GETTING DOWN TO BUSINESS

The Procrastination Problem

There is one thing in the world that every one of us has in equal amounts, and that is time. Procrastination is one of the worst thieves of our time and productivity. If you leave tasks until the last minute, you will have to rush, you won't do your best work, and you will be more stressed.

If you know that you have the tendency to procrastinate, here's a simple method to help you get over the habit. Just make a list. List the tasks you have to complete. List everything, from driving the kids to school to finishing your proposal. List daily tasks and the amount of time they take, and also list long-term tasks and the amount of time you estimate they will take and when they have to be completed. Now break your long-term tasks into smaller, daily time segments and schedule your work into your day. Is your schedule reasonable? You don't want to have every waking moment scheduled, but you do want to make sure that you have allotted enough time each day to work on your long-term tasks. Then you won't find yourself with your back against the wall, trying to do everything at the last minute.

Another problem is that we often procrastinate on the tasks we like the least. If you get into the habit of clearing those items off your schedule first, you'll be done with them, and you won't have to spend so much time fretting and stressing over your dreaded tasks.

HOME BUSINESS PROBLEM #57

THE CORPORATE CAFETERIA IS ALWAYS OPEN!

CHAPTER SIX

Taking Care of Business—Taking Care of Yourself

WAHMs are busy ladies, but don't let that be an excuse for not taking care of yourself. Running a home business can take its toll on a mom. Be careful that you don't run yourself into the ground, while you're running your business and taking care of your family. Supermom is a fictional character. Turn off those voices in your head that tell you what you "should" do. You know better than anyone else what is best for you and your family. Listen to your heart and take care of the most important things.

I'm Alone in Here

My twelve-year-old daughter was recently at a sleepover where someone brought R-rated videos that she knew would give her nightmares. She was torn between wanting to come home and staying. She knew if she left, she'd be labeled a "dork." But if she stayed she wouldn't enjoy herself. She didn't want to feel pressured into doing something she didn't want to do or watching a movie she didn't want to see. At 1:00 A.M. my phone rang.

"Mom, I want to come home," she whispered. "But I don't want my friends to be mad at me."

"This is a perfect opportunity to blame your exit on good old Mom," I said. "Just say what I tell you to say, and you'll have a way out."

"Nicki," I continued, "you must come home right now!" Then I whispered, "Now you say: "But Mom! I don't want to leave.""

Nicki protested, "Mom, what are you doing?"

"Just trust me, Nicki. Do as I say and you'll have an excuse to leave, without looking like a dork."

"But Mom."

"Just say it Nicki!"

"Okay," she agreed. "But Mom," she said weakly, "I don't want to leave."

"You come home right now young lady, I will not allow you to watch that movie!"

"Now you say, 'Come home? Now? But Mom, I want to watch it, let me stay, please!'"

"But Mom," she said, again.

"Nicki," I interrupted her, "just repeat what I tell you, why won't you cooperate?"

"Because Mom," finally I stopped talking long enough to listen. "I'm alone in here."

Do you ever feel alone in here? Working at home, alone, can be isolating. But it doesn't have to be that way. Not only that, you can't let it be that way. No matter what your situation—work-at-home mom, stay at home mom, working mom, . . . you need to continue to make new contacts, meet new friends, new people, all the time. If you want to grow your business and expand your opportunities, expand your own horizons, you need to get out. Physically get out and meet new people or if you live in a rural area, through the Internet.

Challenge yourself to break out of your comfort zone. You may need to go little by little at first. Introduce yourself to a new parent at school, join a club, and sign up for a class with your children. If you think about it, you'll find many ways to meet new people and stay in touch with old friends: through your child's school, at the grocery store, via email, or mailing lists. You never know when you'll make a great new business contact or start a new friendship.

My daughter did decide to come home from the sleepover that night, all on her own. She may have been alone in there while she made her call home, but her good friends were there for her, and they understood. You don't have to feel "alone in here" anymore either. Get out and meet people today.

Take Time for Yourself

Don't give up your hobbies or other things that give you pleasure. If you enjoyed knitting or needlework before you started working at home, keep it up. You might not have as much time to devote to it as you did before, but you don't have to stop entirely either. Just be realistic. Don't try to get a huge project done in a few days or make all of your children's clothes yourself.

If you're artistic, but don't have a hobby, take a painting class or set aside a little time each day to sketch. Keep a sketchbook in your car for the times you're waiting for your children at school or during other activities. Do you play a musical instrument? Play a little each day, just for your own enjoyment, or get together with friends or a community group to make music together.

Nurture your friendships, too. You may be busier than you've ever been, but your friends are still just as important to you; they may be even more important now. It only takes a few minutes to stay in touch. Occasionally invite a friend over for coffee or meet for lunch. Good friends don't care if your floors are waxed or if the carpet is stained; don't let these concerns stop you from enjoying the company of others.

These little sanity breaks keep you happy and motivated.

TIP!

Tylenol for Mom

Just the other day, my daughter was playing a game with one of her friends. Her friend, Emily, gave Nicki clues, trying to get her to say the words "birth certificate."

Emily said, "Okay, this is something your mom was given as soon as you were born, and she'll keep it with her for the rest of your life."

"Tylenol," Nicki answered.

Of course, every mother knows the correct answer is Valium, but she was close.

I was reminded of this as the kids were getting dressed this morning. Socks give me a headache.

My favorite thing about summer is that my kids wear sandals every day and they don't need socks. When that cooler weather sets in, every morning I hear "Mom, where are my socks?"

I don't understand why keeping track of socks is so difficult. My husband never understood the problem, until I lost my patience one day. "Where do all the socks go? How hard can it be to keep track of socks?" he asked. Well Dear, you want to walk a mile in my shoes? I put him in charge of socks.

We set up a base camp in the hallway so I could acclimate him to the laundry room. I wouldn't want him to enter such unfamiliar surroundings too quickly.

His question, "How hard can it be?" is similar to what I hear from many moms who want to work at home. From the outside, working at home looks like the perfect solution. Making money, staying at home, taking care of your own kids—it all sounds so good. And it has been a great a solution for my family and me, but until you walk in my shoes, don't assume working at home is the perfect solution.

A work-at-home mom wears the hats of both a working mother and a stay-at-home mother. There are no sick days and no vacation pay. It's not easy, but I hate to think that my kids see themselves as the source of my next headache. I do my best to be positive and pleasant, and, I find that I'm best able to do that if I'm taking care of myself as well as them.

Now, I don't assume to understand your situation, and I'll be happy to walk a mile in your shoes too . . . as soon as I find my socks!

Serve Your Community

Serving your community may not seem like advice for taking care of yourself, but it is. When I start feeling sorry for myself, or I'm getting whiny, the quickest fix is to do something charitable. I've discovered that it's actually not more giving, it's getting.

SANITY

Teach a class at your church or synagogue. Take the kids to a retirement home once a week just to sit and visit with the residents. Take dinner to a homeless shelter. Clean out your closets and donate all of the clothes your kids have outgrown to a woman's shelter.

We're never as energized as when we're doing something for others.

TIP!

Hey Dad?

For a lot of people, spring is the time of new beginnings, but I think that about fall. The kids are back in school and football season has started. Now I have more time for projects I have planned, more time for ME.

Perhaps I will have time to work on my business, add new features to my site, or work on that writing project. In addition to the time I have once the kids are back in school, I also have more motivation. I love to shop for school supplies. New paper and new pencils seem to motivate me to begin new projects.

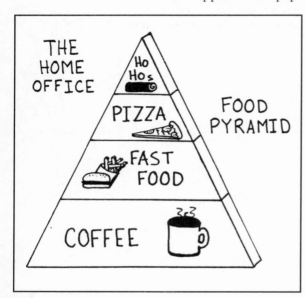

THE HOME OFFICE

Ho Hos

PIZZA

FOOD PYRAMID

FAST FOOD

COFFEE

These were my thoughts in the shower the other day when suddenly my little girl threw back the shower curtain and said, "Hey Dad?"

Now, this is very bad news for:

a. Me, because naked, I look like my husband.

b. My husband, because naked, I look like him.

c. My daughter, for not being able to tell the difference.

The correct answer is probably "all of the above."

Working at home and spending a lot of time on the computer obviously haven't done much for my fitness or shape. I guess my first "me" project should be to get serious about an exercise program.

Maybe that way, the next time I'm interrupted in the shower, there won't be an identity mix-up.

Don't Become Your Own Best Customer

When I was little, I asked my mom why the doughnut man was SO large. She said he was "eating all the profits." I wondered what a profit was, and why he would want to eat so many? If you own a business that sells products, keep track of your personal purchases. If you like the products, allow yourself a certain percentage of your profits for your own purchases. That way you won't get carried away, and like my doughnut man, "eat all your profits."

MONEY SAVING

TIP!

How do you handle sick days?

And sick days are . . . what? I'm not familiar with that term. Seriously, I haven't been sick for a very long time (knock on wood!). If it came to the point where I couldn't work, I would have to make up the time by working late nights and weekends.

Note from Cheryl: If you deal with deadlines in your business, it's a good idea to have a backup plan for sick days. Arrange for help from a neighbor or have your husband come home from work early. If you plan ahead for the possibility of sick days, they won't be as stressful.

When I'm sick, I work if I can. Otherwise I get very grumpy and try to sleep as much as possible while the kids go to the sitter's. When my kids are sick, I lose a lot of work time and enjoy the cuddly time with my kids since that is the only time they like to cuddle.

When I'm sick, I let my kids get away with almost everything—short of bloodshed—in return for their leaving me alone. On those days, they get away with crackers on the couch and endless TV and videos. They eat junk food and instant food all day. It's worth it if they let me rest. I don't sleep, really, but at least it's rest.

I don't handle sick days very well. It's frustrating, because as Mom, the burden all falls on me. My new strategy is that because I am working full-time too—yes from home but still working—my husband must share the responsibility of taking time off from work to care for sick kids when they stay home from school. The children feel as if they're a burden when someone is only half there for them, especially when they are sick. They deserve better than that. They deserve to be treated with TLC—not interrupted by phone calls, faxes, and deadlines.

Actually, in some ways sick days are easier. I'm forced to stay at home—not run all over the country doing little errands that could be left undone. Luckily, my kids tend to sleep most of the day when they are sick. When they are awake, they like to stay still and watch a good movie or drink a cup of soup. I actually get uninterrupted time for my business.

One reason I became a WAHM was because I resented feeling guilty when I had to miss work to stay at home with sick children. I'm a single parent, so this is always my responsibility. Now that I'm a WAHM, the neat part is feeling free enough to be here for my children. I don't have to send them to school when they're not feeling well, either. I've learned to tell my clients when I need to cancel the day's appointments, if necessary.

WE MAKE OUR OWN BREAKFAST WHEN MOM IS SICK... SO SHE WON'T HAVE AS MUCH WORK TO DO.

GETTING DOWN TO BUSINESS

Take a Break

Do you find you're getting frustrated with your business, your husband, or your kids? Is your family happy? Are you happy? Are you staying true to your priorities? Are you taking care of your yourself and your relationships?

If you find that you have nothing but questions and you're not finding any answers, maybe it's time to take a break.

Sometimes the answers are right in front of us. We often discover them when we take the time to be quiet and listen. When was the last time you just sat quietly, with no distractions, no noise? We live in such a hectic world that this isn't easy to do. Yet clearing our minds is sometimes the only way to really hear the answers.

There's always something making noise in our house—TV, radio, even the refrigerator motor. When the power went out for a short time the other day, I was amazed at how quiet the house became. It was wonderful!

If you can manage it, take a longer break and really get away. Take a vacation, even if it's just one night or the weekend, and clear your mind of all business issues. Don't even think about your business, just get away. (If you take your business with you on vacation, you will be a work-on-the-road mom, a WORM, and that doesn't sound good, does it?)

Give it a try. Spend your quiet time praying or meditating, or get away and clear your mind of the distractions of life. You may be surprised at what you are then able to hear.

A Gift from the Sea, by Anne Morrow Lindbergh, is an excellent book to take on vacation. Even though this book was written in 1955, it speaks to today's mothers looking for balance in their lives.

You may find that the answers you have been searching for become obvious. Perhaps you will decide that you are happiest being a part-time WAHM, working at home one or two days each week, or not working at home at all. And if the answer you come up with is that you need to slow down or change your working situation, don't look at it as a failure. No business is worth the sacrifice of your relationship with your family or your husband.

Are you taking care of yourself?

I am practicing the safest form of birth control since my first child was born six months ago—a strong lack of personal hygiene. I have forgotten the feel of bath bubbles on my body. My makeup has long exceeded its expiration date for use. My full nursing breasts have yet to see lace and as for my G-strings . . . well, they are still packed away with my pre-baby day clothes (and I weigh less than I did before baby).

Now, honestly, I have a wonderful husband who is still intrigued with me, even in my current nongender form. But I feel I have allowed the importance of my self to dwindle in comparison to baby, hubby, household management, meals, work, and extended family.

Note from Cheryl: It sounds like it's time to treat yourself to some pampering. Get yourself some bubble bath and a good book and take a break!

My home business is fairly new (three months), so to get off to a good start I was working until 2 or 3 a.m. about four to five nights a week. (I get up around 7 or 8 a.m.) This went on for a few weeks until my youngest started teething and waking up throughout the night. I knew something had to give, so my housecleaning standards went down a few more degrees. As hard as I may try, it is impossible to be superwoman and now I go to bed around midnight.

I have been struggling with this question lately. I do so much for my four children that I was not getting enough exercise. I was upset by my weight gain, and I decided to make some changes. Now I take a half-hour walk each day. I'm starting slowly because it has been so long. This is not just exercise, it's also thinking time, and I've decided I can't live without it.

Now I do. That wasn't always the case. I used to try to be superwoman. But I figured out that I could not be an excellent mom, excellent wife, and excellent small-business owner all at the same time. I had to weigh the importance versus my availability. Now, I go to bed a little earlier and wake up a little earlier. I don't accept every job, even though the money would be great! I won't have forever with my four-year-old; he will be grown and gone soon enough.

So I didn't get that new pair of shoes or that hair cut I desperately need, but I do take a nap with my little boy every day. I wake up at 5 a.m. to start my day so that by the time he wakes up I will be available (for the most part). Now if I could just make him understand that he doesn't have to talk to everyone who calls on the phone, life would be grand!

The bedroom door is closed, the earplugs are on, and my husband's on night duty. I need my eight hours solid sleep and everyone in the family knows it. I need good food, good rest, down time, and quiet moments—complete with candles and soft music. It really is possible to have this every day.

Sleep I get enough of. I'm one of those people who has to have eight hours every night. But I do tend to let other things go. I find I have to force myself to stop working and eat lunch in the kitchen instead of at my desk. I tend to use every waking moment not occupied by my kids for business. My hubby is great because he recognizes this and makes me stop and take time for myself. Just this week he called a sitter (all by himself) and dragged me out of the house for a real date! Movie and dinner, wow! If it weren't for him, I'd probably be glued to the computer day and night!

Do you dress for success or dress to depress?

Dress for success of course. If I don't visualize my own success, I can't materialize my own success.

I do most of my work during my son's naps or late at night after he's in bed. Sometimes, I'm up until 4:30 a.m. So comfort is the key. I wear sweats and slippers.

I am usually up, showered, dressed, and made up before I start my day. It makes me feel professional. I do admit, though, that my attire is a lot more relaxed than when I worked outside the home. No more pantyhose!

I am a professional image consultant, but I do not want to be uncomfortable or intimidating to my clients who come to me for advice. I wear anything from dress jeans and bright sweaters to casual knits with blazers. This way I can still play Candyland on the floor and be ready at a moment's notice for my clients. I am amazed at how many people I see while running errands who assumed I had a traditional career outside the home because I don't "look" like a woman who stays at home with her kids. Moms: put on some makeup and let that ponytail down. You're worth the time it takes!

I must admit that I most closely resemble the "dress to depress." However, it depends on the day of the week. I try to schedule most of my errands and deliveries to two days a week and I dress much better on those days. Other days when I know that I am not going anywhere, comfy sweats are my uniform of choice. I have been "caught" by a client who stopped by unexpectedly and I was wearing my bunny slippers. Oh well, at least he thought it was funny.

Note from Cheryl: I know I joke about it, but your home and your appearance affect how you feel about yourself and how others see you. Take the time to take care of yourself and your home.

CHAPTER SEVEN

Husbands and Home Businesses

Many things will change when you begin working at home, but don't assume that your husband will be one of them. I hope you have a supportive husband, but if you don't, don't give up. Perhaps with a little adjustment in both of your attitudes, he will come around. After all, having a happy wife and family is in his best interest, too. Remind your husband that you share the goal of raising your children to become happy, productive adults. He probably agrees that having them cared for by someone who loves them is the best path to that goal. If so, you're halfway there already.

Husbands

People often ask me what it takes to have a successful home business. Of course everyone is different, but from my own experience and from what I've heard from other moms, having a supportive spouse is a key to success. If your husband doesn't support the idea of your working at home, don't make the mistake of assuming that he will change his mind after you start your business. He may come around if and when you start making money with your business, but there are no guarantees.

Make sure he knows how important working at home is to you and your children. When you're first deciding whether to work at home, calculate together where you can cut expenses. Work together as a team on your daily schedules. These will change as you begin your business and as it grows.

IF THIS IS YOUR HUSBAND	THIS WILL BE YOUR HUSBAND
HONEY, BRING ME A BEER WHEN YOU FINISH THE DISHES	HONEY, BRING ME A BEER WHEN YOU FINISH THE INVOICES
BEFORE YOUR BUSINESS	AFTER YOUR BUSINESS

Demonstrate to your husband how his life may be easier when you are at home. Perhaps he won't have to leave work early to share pick-ups and drop-offs at school and child care, to care for a sick child, or trade sick days with you. You will be available to do that now. If he travels often on business, it won't be as difficult to coordinate your work and child care schedules when he is out of town. Your mornings may be less hectic since you will have control of your own work schedule and you won't have to hurry your children out of the house to child care.

Establish your expectations with your husband before you begin working at home, and continue to communicate with one another as your business grows. Your business isn't worth jeopardizing your relationship, so be sure that you agree on decisions. Of course there will be ups and downs, but common goals and expectations will make the transition easier.

Spending Quality Time with Your Husband Doesn't Have to Be Expensive.

Plan a "date" at home after the kids are in bed. Take advantage of being home during the day and start your children's bedtime routines a little earlier than normal. Have them fed, bathed, and in their pajamas. Then, you can spend a little extra time curling your hair and getting ready for your date. Your children will see that your relationship with your husband is important, too.

Candles, a special dinner, and a rented video can be just as enjoyable as an expensive evening out. Plan ahead and concentrate on making each other feel special.

TIME
SAVING

TIP!

Help Make Dad Time Special

The next time you find a board game or craft kit on sale, consider how much time it will buy you. How much do you pay a babysitter? Five dollars an hour? If a ten dollar board game will buy you hours of uninterrupted work, it's well worth the money. My girls keep their eyes open for games they know Dad will like. NFL Monopoly is a big hit. A model car kit was another popular choice.

If you're not a video game fan, but your husband is, reserve the video game time for Dad. My husband sets up double elimination tournaments for the whole neighborhood, with competition ladders printed on poster board and prize ribbons.

Dad's movie night is another treat my girls look forward to. He chooses a classic movie he wants to introduce them to, maybe an old John Wayne movie or the Three Stooges. They're not movies the kids would choose for themselves, but they always enjoy them. They pop popcorn and Dad tells tales about how movies used to be "back in the old days."

Put together a group of father/daughter or father/son pairs and start a book group. Each pair takes turns choosing a book and hosting a discussion at their home. You can even decorate and serve food that fits the theme of the book you're discussing.

My Sausage

My husband has a way of getting what he wants, only he takes the longest possible route to get there. Last Sunday morning we stopped at McDonald's before church. We had some time to kill because of a little schedule mix-up, but that's another story.

My daughter wanted to order a piece of sausage, so Mike ran in to get it for her. I expected him to come back with a piece of sausage, but no, he came back with a bag full of food. Instead of ordering one piece of sausage (because it wasn't on the menu), he ordered the Sausage Egg McMuffin with Cheese, only he ordered it without cheese, egg, or muffin. The McDonald's worker told him he could get the Sausage Egg McMuffin with Cheese Value Meal for only 20 cents more, and then he could not get hash browns and coffee too.

Finally, he came back to the car and handed the bag to me. By now we had to get back to church. As we drove away, I opened the bag to find: coffee, hash browns, muffin, egg, and cheese, but, you guessed it, no sausage!

Is your home business like my McDonald's bag? Did you start out with a specific purpose, a goal in mind? Such as working from home so you could spend more time with your children? Have you gradually drifted away from your original purpose? Are you so engrossed in your business that you've lost sight of the reason you started working from home in the first place? I know it's easy, even tempting sometimes, to get so caught up in the day-to-day details of working that we forget to pay attention to the things that are really important in our lives.

I've had plenty of days lately when I've had more work than hours. I sometimes have to remind myself of my priorities and rearrange my schedule so I'm here for the kids and here for the things that really matter to me. These memories, the time I have with my husband and girls, the memories we're making together are my "sausage." This is what I want more than anything else, so I give them priority.

I'd hate to work for years, thinking I'm doing the best for my kids and my family, only to find I've ended up with a bag full of hash browns.

Hire Your Family

wahm.com

MONEY
MAKING

If he's willing, enlist your husband's support for your business. Have him carry your business cards or catalogs and pass them out to people who may be interested in your business. Most likely he has access to a completely different circle of people during the day. Make use of his contacts to grow your business. You can also do this with other family members or friends. You may be surprised by how many people want to see you succeed, and they will be happy to help you reach your goals.

Your children can stuff envelopes, fill orders, stamp catalogs, and help with many other home office tasks. Many children enjoy working alongside their mom, and it gives them a sense of ownership in your business. They may be less likely to resent the time you devote to your business if they feel the business belongs to them too.

If you wish to formalize your family's employment, you can pay them wages and deduct their wages as business expenses. There are additional IRS requirements you have to meet when you hire family members, so check your state's employment regulations and check with your accountant for rules that apply.

TIP!

Does your husband support your business?

My husband is supportive of my business, although he believes it should be up to me to make a success of it without too much of his input. It's really helpful that he is a CPA and can give great advice.

My husband is the best. He always supports me in any business venture I look at, because he sees how happy it makes me—and the kids! I work out of the house right now as well as take care of my children. My husband is always there to make sure things run easily for me. When he comes home, he makes sure the kids are occupied so I can finish my work. When it comes to support, he is the best.

Once my husband saw that I could really make money with my business, he became very supportive. I make sure that I tell him all the good business news I get and I show him every check that comes in the mail. Since I've started doing that, he doesn't complain when I need help feeding the kids or cleaning up after supper.

Note from Cheryl: I hear this from a lot of moms. Many husbands become more supportive when their wives start earning money, so be sure to share news of your financial success with him.

YOU KNOW HONEY... IT SEEMS LIKE WE HARDLY EVER HAVE TIME ALONE ANYMORE ...HONEY ??

Basically, my husband supports my business. Sometimes, however, he asks when am I going to "get a job," meaning outside the home. But when we sit down and discuss it, we both agree that my being home is the best decision for our family right now. My husband's work schedule varies every week and he works all shifts. Sometimes he is off during the middle of the week and he takes care of the baby while I work. That is the best form of support I could ask for!

My husband (bless him) has been very supportive. He really gave me the extra push to get my business off the ground. I just had a major accomplishment this week and he told me how proud he was of me. In all honesty, he would rather that I work from home. I'm more relaxed, with less stress. I'm halfway there now. I recently went half time at my outside job. Our goal is for me to work completely from home by this time next year.

Note from Cheryl: Many moms are "transitional WAHMs," slowly moving into the work-at-home lifestyle. This approach is often less stressful for their family and causes less financial strain.

My husband is rather old-fashioned and would rather be the sole breadwinner, like his father. His mother quit working when she had kids and never went back. He doesn't consider what I do "work" as it is not physical labor. (He didn't consider it "work" when it was 9 to 5 in the office either, and now that I'm doing it from home, it is even less like real work to him.) I find he expects me to be doing a lot more of the domestic work since I'm home all the time now. He gets upset when the dishes aren't done, the meals made, or the toys aren't picked up. Kind of like, "what have you been doing all day? Watching soap operas?" It is aggravating, but I know that's just the way he is and he's not going to change. He doesn't complain too much when I get paid.

Note from Cheryl: Again, communication is the key. Talk with each other and work out a schedule. Then look at your daily schedule together and figure out which tasks can get done and which tasks will have to be done later in the day. It will help him see what you're "doing all day."

Now that I'm making money, yes. However, in the beginning when I was just "trying" to make money, he could have been more supportive. He mostly viewed what I was doing as playing on the computer, yet he now realizes that those couple years of work with no pay has now paid off. Now, he's my best salesman.

He's 150 percent behind me! He promotes my business every chance he gets and is my biggest fan. He always encourages me and gives me the necessary boosts. For instance, I've just begun to develop my "local presence" and network in the real world. My husband has been just great with this.

My husband is very supportive of my business. He helps me when he has the time. In fact, he keeps asking me if we've made enough money for him to join me in the business and become a work-at-home dad.

If You're on Your Own

Single moms face unique challenges when running home businesses. It is more difficult if you don't have the support of a spouse, but not impossible. I know many single work-at-home moms. Most of them do have an extended support network, such as family members and neighbors who can help when they're needed.

Many single WAHMs don't work at home full-time because they can't afford to leave their traditional jobs and be without a steady income for any amount of time. Keeping their insurance coverage is another important consideration for single WAHMs. They work their home businesses on the side, keeping their jobs until they can afford to become WAHMs full-time.

Single WAHMs can also use existing child care co-ops or start one of their own. If you know other work-at-home moms in your area, consider trading child care with them so you can each have some uninterrupted time to work. Your children will get to be with their friends, too, as a bonus.

If you live near extended family members, tell them what you are trying to do. Ask them if they can be available from time to time if you need to meet with a client or spend extra time working on a project. You will probably find that many people are supportive of your goal to spend more time with your children and will help you and your business toward success.

wahm.com Husbands and Home Businesses

CHAPTER EIGHT

Children and Home Businesses

"Nothing you do for children is ever wasted."—Garrison Keillor

Running a business while taking care of your children may be challenging, but with planning and self-discipline, it can be accomplished. You and your family will find numerous benefits. You can fulfill your career goals and be a strong role model. You will have quantity time—as well as quality time, with your children.

Remember, your children will grow up before you know it. You will have many years to work and make money, but you can't get their childhood back. Maybe you won't be able to work full-time until your children are older; maybe you won't become president of a company before you're 40. But you will have the memories of the time you've spent with your children. What could be more important than that? People say it takes a village to raise a child, but I know who's raising mine. I am. That's the most important thing to me.

Mixing Children and Business

Some moms choose to keep their business completely separate from their children. They lock their offices up in a separate room and don't let anyone in. Others incorporate their businesses into their family life.

I've found that a blend of both approaches works best with my family. While there are times that I must work without any interruptions, there are other times when I welcome my family's input. My oldest daughter designed all of my website graphics and my youngest suggests ideas for columns and cartoons. For the most part, I work when my kids are at school or sleeping. Sometimes, though, something must be accomplished when they're home. The fact that they're so involved gives them a feeling of ownership in the business and they're less likely to resent the time that I devote to it.

Of course you should consider safety issues when you determine how involved your children can be. If you're making candles, you won't want little ones around the hot wax, but they may be able to help wrap candles or apply labels.

These ideas can help keep everyone happy on those occasions when you have to make phone calls, meet with a client, or just need quiet time.

- Keep a box of "telephone toys" handy. Stock it with special, favorite toys that only come out when you need quiet time.
- Set up a mini-office for your child. Equip it with a keyboard (find an inexpensive nonfunctioning keyboard at a thrift store), a phone, While-You-Were-Out notes, and Post-It Notes. Kids often enjoy playing office while you work.

- Set up dates with dad. My children love to take special trips with dad: a picnic dinner at the park, trips to the toy store (just to look), or a bike ride. And I appreciate the extra quiet time.

- Arrange for a neighborhood teenager to come to your home some afternoons as a mother's helper. He or she can play with your children or help with household chores.

- Share child care with a friend or family member.

- Arrange meetings with clients at a child-friendly place such as a McDonald's with a playground. You can talk while your children play in a safe place.

- Create an arts and crafts area for your children. Supply paints and drawing supplies, modeling clay, and other creative tools. If you set it up in your basement or another part of the house where you don't have to worry about spills, your children can let their creativity go crazy. And you won't go crazy worrying about cleaning it all up.

- Designate your kids' nap or quiet time for making your important phone calls or finishing projects that require all your concentration.

Different things work for different families. Find the mix that's right for you, and you'll find that children and business make for a wonderful combination.

Be Creative with Your Children's Activities

Don't force yourself to fit any traditional motherhood images you have in your mind. If you don't enjoy mommy-and-me toddler play days, don't do them. If preschool TV programs make you ill, turn them off. A visit to an art museum, a sculpture garden, or a music store is at least as interesting for a toddler as sitting and watching another TV show. You will enjoy the mental stimulation, too, and return to work refreshed and energized.

TIP!

It's a Good Thing

Martha Stewart is influencing my daughter. I realized this the other day at the grocery store. She picked up a little vegetable brush and said, "Mom, do you know what this is good for?"

"Well, cleaning vegetables I suppose."

"Yes, of course. But it also helps you iron fringe."

"Iron fringe?"

"Yes. You see, you use this brush to straighten and untangle the fringe and then you apply your iron with just a little bit of steam, and voila! Our fringe is straight and neat again."

"What fringe, Nicki?"

My iron doesn't exactly get a workout and it certainly has never touched fringe. I don't even think we own anything with fringe. She shrugged her shoulders and we proceeded to the produce department. "Oh mom, I know of a delightful recipe for apples. Isn't this just the best time of year for apples?"

"Well sure, I guess so. It's fall and all."

"Yes, as I was saying, I know of a great recipe for baked apples. The thing that makes them truly wonderful is the addition of just a dollop of delightful cream sauce served on the side when you plate the apples."

"Plate the apples? Iron my fringe? Nicki, what has gotten into you?"

THESE DAYS, I MEASURE MY JOB PERFORMANCE IN FEET AND INCHES

Her next words shocked me:

"Well, I didn't want to tell you. I've been watching Martha Stewart, Mom. You should watch too. She really does have great ideas."

Where did I go wrong? I wouldn't even buy Nicki

a play vacuum cleaner when she was little because I didn't want her to get the impression that domestic work would be her lot in life. Now she's watching Martha Stewart?

While other moms are worrying about the influence of MTV and rock videos on their children, I've got Martha Stewart influencing mine.

Kids just have to rebel, don't they?

Pay Attention to Your Customers' Interests and Hobbies

Martha Stewart is a perfect example of someone who has made a business out of traditional etiquette and entertaining. She has made a multimillion-dollar business out of attending to details. Take her lead and make money by paying close attention to your customers' interests.

When you see something you know will be of interest to your customers such as a speaker coming to town, a workshop of interest to them, or an article in a magazine, drop them a short note. They will love the personal attention and will think of you next time they need your product or service.

Make a habit of communicating with your customers (and potential customers) at regular intervals. Keep a database of their birthdays, children's birthdays, and anniversaries. Especially in these email days, handwritten notes will help you stand out from the crowd.

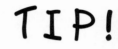

The Back Burner

Moms are always being pulled in several directions at once. You've got your family, your home, and now your home business, all competing for your time and attention. I saw a mom at the video store this weekend. With a girl pulling on her arm saying, "Mom? Mom? Mom? Can I get some candy?" A boy was pulling at her skirt, saying (a little louder than his sister) "MOM? MOM? MOM? Can I rent a video game?" Just then her husband came around the corner and, oblivious to her predicament, innocently asked, "I've narrowed it down to *A Thin Red Line* or *A Simple Plan*. What do you think?" Well, she lost it. She said, in a voice loud enough to draw the attention of everyone in the store,

"Stop it! I can only listen to one of you at a time!"

But then, without missing a beat, she proved herself wrong by answering them all in one breath. She turned to her daughter and said, "Yes, but no gum!" Then turned to her son and said, "Yes, as long as it's not a fighting game."

And finally turned to her husband and said, "No, I want to see *You've Got Mail*."

Yes, moms do have an amazing ability to do so many things at once. But even Supermom can't possibly do everything. If you're like me, I'm guessing there are some things that just don't get done. There are bound to be things that get put on the back burner, chores and tasks you simply don't have time to do.

From time to time, take a closer look at that back burner. Are there tasks that seem to wind up there week after week? Perhaps it's time to get help, or if possible, eliminate those jobs. I find that I usually manage to attend to the things I really enjoy, those that are most important to me. When I look at my back burner, I see jobs that can best be accomplished by someone else or just don't need to be done at all. Maybe the beds won't get made every day. Maybe it's time to say "No" the next time I'm asked to volunteer my time or join a committee.

Maybe someday, I'll get the whole stove cleared off!

MONEY SAVING

Take Advantage of Services in Your Community

Staying at home gives you the freedom to take advantage of many services in your community. You may be surprised by the many inexpensive, enjoyable activities to do with your children:

- Use the public library to check out books, tapes, and magazines.
- Attend story time at the bookstore.
- Pack up a picnic and take the kids to the park or zoo.
- Tour local businesses for a behind-the-scenes peek into their operations.
- Arrange a small field trip with other moms and your children's friends to the fire station, candy shop, pizza shop, artist's studio, or grocery store.

You will find many ways to entertain your family on a shoestring.

TIP!

Bookstores and Alligators

We had spent a little too long at the bookstore the other day, and I was trying to hurry my daughter out the door. If you knew my kids, you would know that they don't do anything quickly. She was slowly making her way toward the exit, jumping from white tile to white tile, carefully avoiding the blue (water) tiles.

As I waited for her by the door, a greeting card caught my eye. It said, "I don't take my problems to work, I leave them at child care."

Maybe that was supposed to be a joke, but it made me sad to think that parents would ever describe their kids as problems. I was brought back to "reality" when my daughter shouted, "Look out, Mom! You almost stepped on an alligator!"

The tiles had apparently transformed themselves into alligator-infested swampland.

I guess this might seem like a problem to some people, a little girl who won't move quickly, a mom in a hurry. But really, what could be more important in my life right now? What could need my attention more than this little girl who has placed herself in the middle of an alligator swamp?

So we hopped and skipped out the door, drawing some strange looks, I'm sure. Strange looks from those who don't know about alligator swamps in the bookstore, or, perhaps more likely, from those who have long since forgotten about them.

Do you ever find yourself saying, "Well, someday, when I have more time I can play with my kids more?" Or, "Someday, when we have more money in the bank, I will be able to spend more time with my family?"

There are times, when a loved one is lost through accident or illness, that we are reminded just how fragile our lives can be. We see someone whose life is cut short, and we remember that life isn't always fair, or predictable.

So be careful that you aren't putting off the really important things in your life, creating problems where there really aren't any . . . and always waiting for someday . . .

Because sometimes, someday doesn't come.

Cheap Fun

If you're trying to cut expenses as you work at home, put your child's imagination to good use. What parent hasn't been frustrated when they've given their child a gift but the child was more interested in playing with the box than the new toy? Children have the most fun with the simplest objects. When you can't beat 'em, join 'em.

- Save the box your computer comes in. If you see a new washer being delivered next door, ask for the box. Set it up in the middle of the playroom, give the kids a set of markers, and you have an instant spaceship, playhouse, or school bus.

- Cut out black and white squares of paper and create a giant chess or checker board. Put the kids to work creating game pieces from household items. One time we made an entire chess set out of juice boxes and soda bottles.

- Have the kids make their own puzzles out of their artwork. Cut the drawings and paintings into simple shapes and store the new puzzles in individual envelopes.

- Rolled newspapers make wonderful building logs. Stack four large sheets of newspaper and roll them together diagonally over a pencil. Tape the log shut and trim the ends so each log is approximately thirty inches long. The logs can be connected in a variety of ways for hours of inexpensive fun.

- Kids can make their own musical instruments out of cast-offs. Oatmeal boxes become drums, pie plates are clangy cymbals, and empty paper towel rolls make natural trumpets.

- Create a craft box with markers, paints, crepe paper, tissue paper, and glue sticks. Children can occupy themselves for hours creating masterpieces.

TIP!

What's Your Title?

It was one of those moments I wanted to freeze in time. I was driving the car and my little girl, Dani, was riding next to me, singing along with Blue's Clues. We were on our way to the mall to pick up my oldest daughter, Nicki. But first, we planned a little side trip to the zoo. I knew Dani would be asking for "cool" music before long, wanting to shop with her friends for clothes and jewelry instead of spending time with Mom. But for now, she was more than happy to be riding along with me.

She interrupted my thoughts, "Mom? Will I always be able to call you Mom?"

"Of course, Dani. What else would you call me?"

"Well, I was just thinking. When I get older, I might have to call you something else."

MY TITLE? WELL ... YOU CAN CALL ME A CEO/ MANAGER / CHAUFFEUR / CHEF / MENTOR / TEACHER ... OR MOM !

What should I call you? It does make a big difference, you know. In your attitude, and how others see you. Are you really taking your business seriously? Do you give yourself credit for all the work you do?

I've talked to a lot of work-at-home moms who have told me that they noticed a difference in their businesses as soon as they gave themselves a title. Instead of minimizing their work, they spoke as if they were already successful. "I'm a writer; I design websites; I'm a painter; I'm a graphic designer; I'm a business owner."

Give yourself credit for everything you do by giving yourself a title. Watch it make a difference for you, too.

We all have many titles in our lives; some change, some don't. I may go back to a "real job" someday, and I may change careers again, but I will always be Mom to my girls.

"Dani," I told her. "Remember when Grandma was here? And Daddy called her Mom? And you said, 'Dad, Mom is in the kitchen, that's Grandma.'"

"Oh yeah, he still calls Grandma Mom . . . so I guess I will always call you Mom."

"As long as you'll always be my Baby, I'll always be your Mom."

She agreed.

Creative Cooperation

Children seem to have a way of sensing our stress and reacting in the least appropriate manner. If you are in a hurry to get out the door, they drag their feet even more. If you need to talk on the phone for a few uninterrupted minutes, the kids just have to talk to you right now. So take a deep breath, try to relax, and use some creative ways to ease the tension and get more cooperation from your little helpers.

- **Place a singing "spell" on the family.** Statements and requests can only be sung, never spoken. The catch is that each family member has to sing in a different style. Try opera, country, rock, and show tunes. My five-year-old is hilarious when she has to sing in Spice Girls style. She sings, "I'll tell you what I want, what I really really want. A juice box is what I want, what I really really want."

- **Become another family member.** Mom acts like the baby, the five-year-old "becomes" Dad, and big sister and little sister switch personalities. It's not only fun for everyone, but it's fascinating to hear your words coming out of your child's mouth. You will all gain a better understanding of what others are really hearing when you talk to them.

- **Turn on the VCR. No, not to watch a tape.** Turn it on in your real life. Hit rewind when the kids are arguing. Have them run the disagreement in reverse, then push play and have them give it a try again in real-time. Push fast-forward and everyone has to move double-time. Slow motion races are great for getting everyone out the door in record time, believe it or not. Speak, run, and fall down in slow motion. Give it a try; the sillier the better.

- **Learn sign language.** Start with the alphabet so you can finger-spell simple words. You will be surprised at how quickly your children pick it up. Just learn one new letter a day and you will have the whole alphabet memorized in less than a month. Then move on to signs for common words. Babies can even learn signs before they talk. It comes in handy when you're on the phone, and it's also great when you have to communicate across a noisy room.

Mother-Daughter Communication

My daughter has never spoken a single word to me without first reciting:

"Mom . . . Mom . . . Mom . . . Mom . . ."

until I say, "Yes?"

"Do you know what?"

And then she waits for me to say, "What?"

After all of that (if she's remembered what she first came to tell me) she begins her story.

I love it that she so willingly shares her thoughts with me, and I occasionally have to remind myself that whatever she's telling me is important to her. I need to stop what I'm doing and really listen. I'm thankful that I'm home to listen to her when she is ready to talk. I know it won't be long before I descend from the mountain of "My Mom Knows Everything" into the valley of "My Mom is Driving Me Crazy!" I know these days will pass all too quickly, and I'll be wishing I could hear

"Mom . . . Mom . . . Mom . . . Mom" again.

I'm not too old to remember the things my own mom said that drove me crazy. I remember the way she would wait up for me at night. When she finally heard the door open, she called out from her bedroom,

"Is that you?"

"Yea, Mom, I'm home."

It drove me crazy. Can you name one person in the world that could answer "No" to that question? "Is that you?" Who else could it be?

Now, though, I think back on those days and I can identify with my mother. In fact, sometimes I think I'm channeling her. Her words come out of my mouth before I even realize what I'm saying.

The mother of a dear friend of mine passed away unexpectedly last year. When I called my friend, she was going over and over her last conversation with her mother.

"I'm pretty sure I said 'I love you' when I said good-bye, but I'm not sure," she said.

She so wanted to know that those were the last words that had passed between them.

But as mothers we know that we say "I love you" in many ways, from "Be careful" to "What do you see in him?" and yes, even in "Is that you?" I'm sure their last words to each other were "I love you," spoken or not.

And what I would give now to hear my mom call out, "Is that you?" when I walk in the front door of my home. In fact, my vision of heaven is that when I open those pearly gates, I'll hear my mom call out . . .

"Is that you?"

And I'll say, "Yeah Mom, I'm home."

One last time.

What do your children think of your business?

My family is very supportive of my business because I get them involved. My oldest daughter recruits new business; my youngest daughter helps me stamp and prepare my new catalog and separate orders. The baby only tries to climb into the boxes, so he has some training left!

Most of the time it's oh so cool! But when the demands start too early or I work too late, the kids are the first to complain! I just remind them that other kids are alone at home while their parents meet deadlines out at the office. We are careful to make "dates" out alone after I meet those deadlines. I think they like to think they "know what I do" because they watch me work on the computer and phone. I was tickled when my daughter asked from the tub one night "Mom, if your business is still around when I grow up, can I take over?" WOW, what a dream that would be for me.

My kids love the fact that my home business allows us more time together. I never miss school plays or music programs, and I don't need a boss's permission to go. My kids have told me that even on the WORST days, when I'm so busy that I rush through sandwich-making for their lunch and toss them a bag of chips, they'd rather have it this way than be at child care every day. They support me because we're all much happier this way. I'm here to soothe hurt feelings, bandage scraped knees, and share their little joys throughout each day. If I'm on the phone with a client, they've learned to quietly show me or write me a note to slip in front of me. We don't have it all perfected, but we're getting there!

My children are teenagers now, so I think they might like it better if they were home alone each afternoon. I see too many of their peers getting in trouble after school, though, so I'm glad I'm home. I actually think that teenagers need a parent at home even more than younger children do.

My children love my business. I sell toys, so not only am I able to keep my kids my top priority, they are able to play with all the great products that I use for demos. The only fear my oldest son has is that I won't bring all the toys back to him. When I come home from a demonstration, the first thing he looks for is the Toy Box.

I have two businesses: I type for an architectural firm and have a new kitchen tools business. My kids don't mind the typing since I only do that when they are in bed. They sometimes grumble about the new business because it has different time requirements, but once-a-week evenings with Daddy mean pizza and a movie! They all agree it is all much better than when I "went to work."

As I am just starting my own business, my eleven-year-old really hasn't had too much to complain about (other than that I hog the computer!). His number-one concern when I explained to him what I was going to do (start a home business) and why (so I could be at home for him and his two-year-old brother) was whether or not I was going to "make tons of money"!

Do you have a love-hate relationship with your TV? Is it off-limits or your babysitter?

We've been TV abusers for five years. On average the TV is on three to seven hours a day. Sad but true. We definitely need a twelve-step program. I wonder if there's a video that could help us? Just kidding!

Note from Cheryl: There's a lot of controversy regarding how much TV time is too much for children. Personally, my children watch one or two educational programs or a video each day. I think you just need to be careful that you don't start depending on TV to keep your children occupied, or let TV take over your time with your children.

It all depends on the day. During the summer, my kids like to get up early and watch cartoons for about an hour before they eat and get dressed. After that, TV is usually off until evening. They are allowed an hour of TV before bed (if there is anything appropriate on). However, on rainy, snowy, or extremely hot or cold days when the kids can't go outside, they get to watch one movie during the day. That is a big treat for them and they love it. If we know tomorrow will be an inside day, we rent a movie they haven't seen yet.

I don't think the TV is ever off in my house! If I need to get something done, I let my two-year-old pick a video. Nothing works with the older two boys. My husband is even worse than the boys. I would love to get rid of the TV, but I seem to be the only one in the family who does. School will start soon. I will try to regain my sanity then. Right now, the summer has been too long to care.

My daughter is only seventeen months old, but I am already monitoring the amount of time the TV is on. I grew up with limited hours in front of the TV. My parents felt there were more creative and thought-provoking ways to spend a few hours, and I agree. I plan to let my daughter watch only educational TV and some children's videos. I would like my daughter to learn and be entertained in other ways-sports, board games, friendships, volunteering, music, books, family discussion, after-school activities, computers, children's parties, traveling, and museums.

wahm.com
READERS

At our house this summer we turned our TV off. This was my first summer of being a WAHM and I did not know what to expect. We set a goal and I will say that we were approximately 80 percent successful. My three boys ages, twelve, seven, five, spent a summer learning to get along without the TV to entertain. They played board games, read to each other, and spent a lot of time outdoors.

How do you handle business phone calls?

Business calls are still a real challenge for me as my girls are only three and five but we are working on it! Many I can do after bedtime or when Dad is around to take over. Then, I hide in my office with the cordless! Another thing that helps is to quietly explain to my five-year-old that Mommy is working and will take care of things after the phone call is over. A business associate of mine has taught her seven-year-old that if he interrupts her while she is on the phone, she will ALWAYS turn down his request so now he writes it on a piece of paper. She says Yes much more often!

Handling a phone call all depends on what is happening around your house at the moment it rings. My children are usually good. They know when I say, "It is Mommy's business line," and they usually quiet down. I am also fortunate to own a business that deals with children and so all my clients have children and understand. If one of my kids comes into the room screaming while I am on the phone, the client is usually understanding.

I usually try to talk to the kids if they're near before I pick up the receiver and ask them to please be quiet while I'm on the phone. Of course, they usually take this as a cue to eat desserts from the freezer or else pull all the cushions off the sofa and build a fort! If it's an important call and the noise is unbearable, I ask to return the call at another time. Most of my contacts are moms themselves and are pretty understanding.

CHAPTER NINE

Promoting Your Business

Even if you have the best product or service in the world, you won't get sales or make money if no one knows about it. For success, you must get the word out and promote yourself and your business every day.

Promoting Your Business, Promoting Yourself

Business owners are often surprised to find that they have the perfect office setup, they're organized, and everything is in place to start filling orders. Only the phone is not ringing and customers are not lining up to purchase their products. You have to get out there and let people know what you're doing or you will never make a sale.

Self-promotion is not always easy, and it seems to be especially difficult for women. We have been taught that we should be modest and polite, not blow our own horns. Well, without some horn blowing, no one will know about your business. These tips will help you overcome your reluctance and announce your business to the world.

- Use email to promote your business. You don't want to send unsolicited email to strangers. Start with people you know, people who will be pleased to hear about your new endeavor. Ask them to forward the information to anyone they know who might be interested.

- Become an online expert. Set up your own business website and feature articles you've written about your business. For example, if you have an interior design business, post articles about finding a decorator that matches your personality or decorating on a budget. Since other websites are always looking for good content, many will publish your articles. For payment, they will print a bio paragraph about you with a link to your website. If it's not obvious how to submit to a site, write to the publisher and ask if they are open to receiving email submissions. There are other sites that bring together writers and publishers who are looking for content. For example, Idea Marketers at www.ideamarketers.com is used by publishers when they're searching for subject-specific content. Their service is free to writers. You just post your writing and publishers contact you when they want to use your article.

- If you have a website for your business, offer reciprocal links to other related sites. You will provide relevant links to your visitors and their visitors will be able to find you and your business. This way, you can work together with other sites to increase the traffic to all of your sites.

- Paper Direct (800-272-7377/www.paperdirect.com) and other creative paper sources sell high-quality preprinted paper stock. With these, you can create brochures and sales letters that are sure to make a good impression without costing a fortune.

- Attend a convention or trade show geared to your target market. Not only will you meet potential customers, you will also meet other business people with whom you can network as you grow your business.

- Create a speech or presentation to present to area community groups. You will be providing them with valuable information and you will get more recognition (and publicity) for your business. Be sure to promote your appearance on your website and in the local paper.

- Join your local chamber of commerce or other small business organizations to network and work with other business owners.

- Use SCORE , the Service Corps of Retired Executives. SCORE is a nonprofit association of retired executives and former small business owners who volunteer their time. They are dedicated to entrepreneur education and the formation, growth, and success of small business nationwide. Volunteers offer free counseling to business owners and now they even offer email counseling. Find a chapter near you through their website at: www.score.org, or call 800-634-0245.

When you start following these tips, your phone should start ringing!

What Do I Get?

As we were preparing to celebrate Stay Home With Your Kids Day this year, I told my girls, "Stay Home with Your Kids Day is coming up."

"Yay! What do we get?"

My response was, "Well . . . you get . . . ME! All day!"

I could tell by their expressions that this wasn't the answer they had hoped to hear.

As adults we try to suppress this natural "What's in it for me?" tendency. But I think deep down, when we hear about something new, we all think, "What do I get?"

When you're promoting your business, do you think first of the clients, the people you can help with your product or service? Or do you think, "What do I get?" We all tell our kids that they have to think of others first. How many times have you told them as the holidays approach, "It's better to give than to receive"?

Are you following your own advice?

If you approach your business with this generous attitude, you will have a better chance of success. Can you describe your business to someone in terms of what you give? Think about it. When asked about your business, do you speak about the products you provide, the service you give to others? Or do you jump right to the commission plan?

Think about what you are "giving" first, and the "getting" will follow.

After I had explained the concept of celebrating our day together, I let my kids choose our activities. They decided that I would play Nintendo with them, and we met their dad for pizza at lunchtime. We watched a few cartoons and then baked a cake together. They convinced me we couldn't have a celebration without a cake. All in all, it was a pretty typical day, except it was special because we celebrated the fact that because I'm working from home, we're able to be together all day, every day.

As we were getting ready for bed, my younger daughter, Dani, said, "I wish tomorrow was Stay Home with Your Kids Day, too."

I just smiled and thought, "It is Dani, it is."

MONEY MAKING

TIP!

Using Press Releases to Promote Your Business

Press releases are among the best ways to get recognition for your business without spending a lot of money. Journalists are always looking for human interest stories and stories about new businesses in the community. By sending your information to them, you're making their job easier. But you should be aware that hundreds of press releases are sent to news professionals every day. You need an angle that will make your release stand out from the rest. The following guidelines can help you find and use that angle.

First of all, press releases should be newsworthy. Watch, read, and listen to the news. Is there a hot topic currently in the news relating to your business? For example, if there are stories about high gasoline prices, focus your story on the money-saving alternative to commuting: working at home. There are ways to position your ideas to make even a simple story into a news story.

Pay attention to the editor or producer who works on stories related to your subject. If you can't find the appropriate contact person, call and ask to whom you should address your press release. If you are sending your release to coincide with a holiday or certain time of year, send it several weeks in advance of the date.

Another secret with the press is to follow up with your contact. Be brief but professional and ask if they have any questions about your release. News people work with tight deadlines in hectic environments. Don't waste their time, but let them know that you are available to answer questions or provide more information. Most of the time, you'll reach their voice mail, so prepare a short two-sentence message before you call. Even if you do get a live person, you'll be prepared to talk with enthusiasm about your topic.

Also consider taking a community college or public information class on public relations. If you have PR money in your budget, hire a PR professional or barter with a PR WAHM. Getting the details right can make the difference in whether your story ends up in the wastebasket or in the newspaper.

In appendix D, I've included a press release from WAHM.com that you can customize with your own business information and send out to local media. WAHM.com readers have shared great success stories about this approach. They have been featured in their local newspapers and radio shows, and a few even had TV crews come to their home!

wahm.com

It's All in the Packaging

My girls have one odd restaurant habit. They tend to freak out when the server doesn't understand that they want exactly what they've ordered. If there's a Cheeseburger Deluxe on the menu, one daughter will insist on ordering the Cheeseburger Deluxe, except . . . no onions, no cheese, no lettuce, no tomato, no ketchup, no mayonnaise, no mustard, and no sesame seeds on the bun.

"So, you want a plain hamburger?" the poor unsuspecting waitress will ask.

That's all it takes. "No! No! No!" she'll say. "I want the Cheeseburger Deluxe! With NOTHING ON IT!!"

Or, when asked what she would like to drink, one daughter will say, "You know root beer floats? Well, that's what I want, except . . . I don't want ice cream in it."

"So, you just want a glass of root beer?"

"No! No! No! I want a root beer float! Except NO ICE CREAM!!"

They both do it, and I guess it's probably my fault (like everything else.) Last summer, we were checking out the department store sale ads in the newspaper. I saw a cute Calvin Klein bathing suit in an ad, and soon we were all at the mall, picking out suits.

We found a few nice suits, but not the Calvin Klein number from the ad. We set up base camp in a fitting room and I started trying on suits.

"How are we doing?" I heard the saleswoman ask. I knew she was approaching our booth.

"To your positions girls!" .

I have my girls trained to take their positions at fitting room doors, like armed guards, whenever we hear a saleswoman coming near. It never fails that a saleswoman will try to poke her head in the door just as I'm squeezing into a suit.

They successfully blocked her entry.

"I'd like to try on the Calvin Klein suit, please. The one that's in the newspaper ad," I shout through the door. "Except . . . I'd like it in black, with a control panel on the tummy, extra support, under-wire cups, and a skirt to cover my thighs."

"So, you want the Big Mama Minimizer Suit?"

"No! No! No! I want the Calvin Klein suit!" I repeated. "Hello? What does it take to get service around here?"

You see, it's all in the packaging. Who would want a plain hamburger, when you could have the Cheeseburger Deluxe?

My kids won't eat scrambled eggs, but add a little green food coloring and they devour "green eggs and ham." They won't eat oatmeal, but add a little honey and we're eating porridge, just like the three bears.

Everyone is like this, I'm convinced. We all want to feel special.

Are you taking advantage of this in your business? Are you making each customer feel special? Are you giving them plain burgers or the Cheeseburger Deluxe?

You might have the best product on the market, but if you sell it with a plain wrapper, you'll never reach your full potential.

I was thinking about this the other night when we were out for family pizza night. My daughter ordered the Pepperoni Pizzazz Pizza, except . . . no pepperoni.

"Oh, no," I held my breath. "Don't say it," I thought.

"So, you want a plain cheese pizza then?"

Here we go again . . .

MONEY MAKING

Keep Your Customers Happy

It's the little things that make the difference between a business and a successful business. Keeping your customers happy will go a long way to making your business successful.

- Call your customers or send a personal note or gift certificate just to thank them for their business.

- Give your customers free advertising by featuring their business on your website or in your newsletter.

- Throw a party or informal gathering to network and meet new business people in your community. Set up get-togethers with your work-at-home customers at a coffee shop or in your home. Hire a neighborhood teenager to entertain their children while you visit.

- When you make presentations to local groups, offer to make your customers' advertising materials or newsletters available to the audience.

- Happy customers can be your best advertisers. Don't be afraid to ask them to refer you to their friends and acquaintances who may need products or services. Give your existing customers a small gift or dinner certificate to thank them for each new customer they refer to you.

Remember, it takes twice as long and costs a lot more to get a new customer than to increase sales with a current customer. If you keep your customers happy, they'll keep you in business.

TIP!

The Grass is Always Greener ... or ... Mom? Can We Eat at the Neighbor's House?

My daughters turn up their noses at any food I serve them that doesn't come with a toy or have a cartoon character on the box. It's so frustrating. I imagine I've come up with something they'll like, buy all the ingredients, cook a special dinner and then they won't even taste it.

If they tasted it and then rejected it, I could take that as a critique of my cooking. But they won't even taste anything new—that is, in our house. Send them to a neighbor's or their friend's house and they turn into Julia Child.

WHAT? NO TOY? AND YOU CALL THIS DINNER?

The other day my neighbor said she was grilling seafood and invited the girls over for dinner. I kind of smirked and said, "Sure, but I doubt if they'll eat much more than a piece of white bread. They aren't very adventurous when it comes to food."

"Well," she smirked back at me, "we'll see."

Later, when the girls got home, they started to tell me about their dinner, but I interrupted: "Right, I know what was served, but tell me, what did you actually eat?"

"Well, we started with salmon stuffed tomatoes, followed by grilled tuna steaks. They were so good! You should try them, Mom."

All I could say was, "Who are you and what have you done with my children?"

I guess it's the old "the grass is always greener" story. For some reason, nothing home grown seems as intriguing or wonderful as what's happening or served somewhere else. Are you doing this with your home business? Do you look at other work-at-home moms, and think "I wish my business was like that"? Does it seem like everyone else is doing great things? Do you look at other sites and businesses with envy?

Remember that your business reflects you and your personality. You really wouldn't want it to be like someone else's, would you? How boring that would be, if we were all alike. Take pride in your uniqueness, your special style and way of doing things. You will find a way to be successful, and you can be proud that you did it in your own way.

It might be tuna casserole instead of grilled tuna steaks, but one is not necessarily better than the other. The important thing is, it's your tuna casserole, and that alone makes it special.

Include Your Children in Your Merchandising

Have you noticed that the expensive sugar-coated cereal is always at eye-level for children? That's no accident. Companies know who influences children's purchases; children do, and they market to them.

So if you're selling children's products, pay attention to what appeals to your children. Notice what attracts them and ask their help when setting up displays. Solicit their opinions, even set up mini focus groups with friends and their children. Try out different marketing methods and products with the focus group. They can give clues about what is most appealing.

Include your children in your promotions and use their testimonials—in their own words—in your advertising. Many potential customers are in favor of parents staying home to raise their own children. They will be pleased to support a business that helps make that possible.

Use your experience with your children to market to all children.

Money, Money, Money

If life could only be as easy as my five-year-old imagines it to be. The way she sees it, if we're near an ATM, we're near money. In her world, the ATMs are a source of endless cash.

For those of us in the adult world, it's not so easy. Money worries can be overwhelming. Almost any marriage counselor will tell you that money is the number one cause of arguments and ongoing stress for most couples.

I recently heard from a work-at-home mom wondering about a rumor she heard. According to the rumor, there is a clinic somewhere that will pay $50,000 for a testicle. How would you like to sit in on that family meeting? "Honey? You know how we're getting behind on our bills? Well . . . I think I've found a solution."

Seriously, if you need more money (and who doesn't?), I figure there are two options: make more money or spend less money.

Let's look at making money first. I know it's frustrating to be working and working, and still see little return. Don't give up. If you talk to any successful businessperson, they will most likely tell you that many lean years finally led to years in which they finally made money. On the other hand, don't assume money will eventually come to you automatically.

Be honest with yourself. Are you really "working" your home business? Money won't start rolling in just because you have put your site online or signed up for a business. You need to promote yourself and your business. For success, you must get out there and connect with people. Only then will you be able to listen to the feedback from your customers and act on their suggestions and comments.

I wish this book contained a magic make-money formula. I wish I knew one! I assure you, there is no such thing. However, if you work hard at your business and promote yourself, I believe you will see results.

On the spending less side, there are several resources where you can find helpful advice.

Online

Frugal Moms offers practical, real-world advice: www.frugalmoms.com.

Thankfully, this site doesn't tell you that you have to wash out your Baggies in order to send your kids to college. You will find practical tips for cutting your grocery bills, frugal decorating ideas, and other tips for cutting household expenses. There are also opportunities to meet and share ideas with other frugal moms.

The Dollar Stretcher is another helpful site, www.stretcher.com

This site includes links to freebies, discounts, and a large library of money-saving articles.

Finally, you need to know how to invest the money you're saving. Suze Orman, author of *The Courage to Be Rich,* has many resources on her site, www.suzeorman.com. Here you can learn the basics of investing, how to manage credit, learn about saving for your retirement, and tax information.

Books

Your library should have these books, all of which offer sound suggestions.

The Complete Tightwad Gazette III by Amy Dacyczyn. (Random House, 1997.)

Miserly Moms by Jonni McCoy. (Holly Hall Publishing, 1996.)

Mary Hunt's The Complete Cheapskate by Mary Hunt. (Broadman & Holman Publishers, 1999.)

These few should get you started, and they can lead you to many more helpful resources.

And please, before you do anything desperate, make sure you've done everything possible to reduce your expenses and maximize your income.

Although, I have been thinking. If we could get $50,000 for one testicle, I wonder what they'd give us for the "whole package"?

Use Cross-Promotion to Maximize Your Ad Dollars

Cross-promotion is based on the old saying, "I'll scratch your back if you scratch mine." Find businesses that complement yours and share advertising with them to expand both businesses' customer base. For example, if you have a business selling toys, share advertising with home child care providers.

Are parents potential customers? Put together coloring kits that include your business information and offer them to local restaurants. They will offer them to families with small children. While they're waiting for their meals, the children will stay busy and happy and the parents will find out about your business.

Do you send orders through the mail? Join with several other businesses that also mail products to your target market and include each other's ads with your shipments.

Working with other business not only saves advertising dollars, it enables you to meet other business people in your community and increases your networking contacts.

TIP!

Good Bagels

One day, when my daughter was three, I took her out for breakfast. We stopped at a bakery and bought milk, coffee, and a couple of treats. As she ate her "breakfast" she said, "Mom, this is the best bagel I've ever had!" I started to correct her, to tell her that these weren't bagels at all, but a new thing called doughnuts . . . but then I decided not to. Maybe I would let her go on for awhile longer, thinking that these "good bagels" were a great new discovery. Now, a year later, instead of changing her vocabulary, we all call doughnuts "good bagels."

Labels may not seem important on the surface, but how many times have you described yourself as "just a mom"? Be careful that you don't diminish your role as a mom, and if you're a WAHM, as a businesswoman, too. We're breaking new ground here. Not many people are aware of the opportunities for working from home, or what a great solution it can be for families today.

When people ask "What do you do?" or "Do you work?" do you find yourself at a loss for words? Prepare an answer to have ready. These questions become great opportunities to enlighten others about the wonderful world of working at home. One mom I know met her business partner as a result of her quick response to such a situation. She was attending her son's baseball game when another mom rushed up to catch the final inning. "You're so lucky you don't have to work," she told my friend. "I can never get to these games on time." Instead of getting angry or defensive, my friend simply replied, "Oh, but I do work. I run a custom furniture business from my home." It turned out the other mom was a marketing specialist wrestling with whether or not to quit her job. Intrigued by my friend's business, she started asking questions. They soon teamed up, combining the artistic talents of one mom with the sales and marketing expertise of the other, to create a successful business.

To an outsider, it may appear that you have loads of free time. After all, you are home all day. How many people know about the frenzy of activity that goes on behind closed doors? With the Internet, we're able to communicate with people all over the world. There are moms who are running huge businesses from their homes, but on the surface they appear to be "just moms."

So, if you're a WAHM, don't be afraid to claim your title. You're a businesswoman, a business owner. Because, like it or not, labels do matter. They have an effect on our self-image and influence the opinions of those we meet.

A rose by any other name may smell as sweet, and a doughnut doesn't become health food just by calling it a bagel. But a work-at-home mom deserves all the credit she can get. So wear your label proudly—Mom, WAHM, whatever you prefer—you deserve it!

How do you promote your business? What works best for you?

I've been a freelance writer for four years now. I have never advertised. Almost all of my original work came from a well-written direct mail letter (preceded by phone calls to the company to get a name for the envelope). I have never paid for advertising, because so far, I haven't had to.

When I do trade shows, I give away little trinkets, magnets, pencils, and buttons that have my business and phone number on them. The freebies attract people to my booth so I have time to talk to them about my products. And even if they don't buy then, they have my name and number with them when they do decide to order later.

Networking, networking, networking! Word of mouth is the best. I also highly recommend joining your local Chamber of Commerce, and get involved.

I have magnetic advertising signs on my car doors that include my phone number. I have a housekeeping business, so people see my signs when I'm at a customer's house. They ask the customer if they're happy with my service and then they call me. I drive my advertising!

I sell products through a party plan, and the best promotion for me is talking to the party guests about hosting a show themselves. I also talk to them about becoming a consultant. All of my preparation work is done by really working with the hostess and getting to know her and what she likes and how she would like the show to go. She in turn advertises me without any more work from me. It's pretty easy, too, if I work with my hostess—she's the key!

CHAPTER TEN

Motivation

I recently came across another meaning for the WAHM acronym: "Why does this Always Happen to Me?" Many moms are disappointed once they reach their dream of working at home only to find that their days aren't all wine and roses. It's just not reality. Expect that you will have ups and downs, all the time. That is normal and necessary. How you deal with the ups and downs will determine how successful you will be in the long run.

Oprah Calling

I often wonder if other work-at-home moms share my home business fantasies. Most of the time, my feet are firmly planted on the ground. I have my business plan, I work hard each day, and, slowly, I make progress toward my goals.

But there are days when I imagine that the next phone call will be a publisher calling with a great book deal, or a big investing group calling to ask where they should send the check. Now, not all of my fantasies are this good, mind you. I have my down days, too. Some days I'm sure that this will never work out and that there will never be another visitor to my website. I will look back years from now and wonder why I ever devoted so much time and energy to such a losing proposition.

So I decide that I need a break. To cheer myself up, I pack up the car and the kids and we head to the zoo for the day. We eat junk food and stroll around and just waste time in general.

But then I start thinking about my business again. I fantasize that while I'm gone, Oprah will call, but I won't be home. She will leave a message saying that they're looking for a woman to talk about work-at-home moms on her show, and they would love to have me come to Chicago, but I have to call her back before 5:00 that day, or they will call someone else. And I don't get the message until late that night because I've decided to take the girls to the zoo for the day. There we are, having a great time at the zoo, but I can't stop thinking about Oprah. So I start to get a little panicked, and I call voice mail, just to check.

But, there aren't any messages, and of course there really aren't any messages from Oprah or her producers, so I hang up and think about what a dork I am.

I don't think I'm alone in my fantasies. At least I hope not. From the conversations I've had with other work-at-home moms, these ups and downs are pretty common. The fantasies just seem to be a part of being self-employed. If you're someone who is deciding whether a home business is right for you, keep this in mind. You won't have many routine, boring days in front of you. It can be a roller coaster, this home business lifestyle, but I'm willing to stay put for the ride. In fact, I prefer it. So if you think you're up for a few laps on the coaster, buy your ticket and join us. I don't think you'll regret it.

(Memo to Oprah, you can call anytime!)

Believe it or not, just a few weeks after I wrote this, the unbelievable actually happened . . . Read on.

Oprah Called!

What a week.

Last Wednesday, at about 3:00, the phone rang.

"Cheryl? This is John Doe (names cleverly changed to protect the innocent) from the Oprah show."

I'm not kidding, it really was Oprah's show, calling me! Can you believe it?

We talked about WAHM.com for awhile and then he said,

"Don't get excited, but would you like to share your story with Oprah, and are you available next Tuesday?"

Don't get excited? That's like saying "Eat this coconut cream pie but don't gain weight."

Of course I was available. I didn't mention that we were actually planning a trip to Disneyland. "Hey kids, Chicago can be fun too!" I hung up with the understanding that this was all very up in the air, but a possibility.

After I was off the phone I started jumping around the house and screaming "That was Oprah! That was Oprah!" My four-year-old hid behind the couch and my twelve-year-old was nonchalant. "Yeah? So?" I guess she's always believed me when I've told her "I'm going to be on Oprah someday." Of course, Oprah would call; isn't that what Mom always said would happen? I even had an outfit pre-selected.

We went shopping and I bought the Oprah outfit and got my hair cut. I wanted to be ready if we went to Chicago. And then I waited, and waited. After a couple days it became apparent that I wasn't going to be on the show after all. We continued with our Disney vacation plans, taking Chicago clothes with us just in case, and I continued to call home to check messages.

My Oprah contact did call back and said that they had enough people for the show but liked my story and might be able to work it into a future show. I don't know if that is the standard brush-off or if I still have a chance, but it was certainly exciting while it lasted.

We had a great time at Disneyland and we're home again. Now, I've returned the outfit. It cost more than we usually spend on groceries each month, and it's not the kind of thing I wear around the house anyway.

But . . . looking back, all I can say is . . . I'm so disappointed.

Now, if I was Tony Robbins, or a great motivator, this is when I'd flash a huge smile and say, "But did that get me down? NO! I don't let a little disappointment get ME down. I picked myself up and brushed myself off and the next day I made a million dollars and Barbara Walters called!"

But I'm not Tony, I'm Cheryl. I wish I had a great story to tell you. How to get over disappointments in your business, how to keep going when things aren't going well. I wish I had some insight into staying motivated after a let down. But I'm not in the mood right now.

I want to sleep until noon, then get up and watch All My Children while eating a banana split and drinking a margarita and then go back to bed.

Maybe I'll have a motivational speech for you another day, but right now I have to run out to the store. We're getting low on chocolate syrup.

Visualize Your Success

What are your goals? Be specific. Do you dream of buying a new car with your home business income, or maybe a new house? Do you hope to put your children through college, or see your book of poetry published? Write down your goals; keep a success journal.

Now visualize yourself reaching your goals. In your mind, sign the paperwork, shake hands with the agent, and turn the key to the front door of your new home. Picture yourself sitting in the audience as your child walks across the stage to receive his diploma. See yourself sitting at a book signing, greeting your readers, and granting interviews. The more details, the more real you can make it, the better.

Think of it as practicing for your success, and you know what they say about practice.

TIP!

I Love the Talking

I feel like I'm on a roller coaster sometimes. WAHM.com gets a good review and I'm on cloud nine. The bills start to pile up and I'm ready to throw in the towel. My hit counter reaches a new high, and I'm high right along with it. My kids whine about all the things they want for Christmas and I consider getting a "real job." All I want for Christmas is a best-selling book and hundreds of thousands of new WAHM.com visitors. Is that too much to ask? Well, guess what, Cheryl; there is no Santa Claus. None of this will fall in my lap without a lot of hard work. Is it worth it?

The other night I was lying in bed with my youngest daughter. We always spend time together at bedtime, reading and talking about the day. She pulled the blankets up so it felt like we were in a tent. I told her,

"Dani, I just love being your mom."

And she said, "Mom, I just love being your little girl."

"What is the best thing about being my little girl?" I asked her.

"I love the talking, Mom," she replied.

Her statement reminded me again why I'm doing this. She doesn't need fancy trips and toys; she needs my time. So I keep working away, fitting in my home business work when I can, and concentrating my time on my girls. I will be successful, because I will not give up.

I printed out a sign to hang above my computer. I can look at it on those late nights when the house is asleep and I'm up working. When I'd rather be sleeping, when the house is a mess, when I'm faced with a pile of bills. It reads:

"I love the talking, Mom."

Be the Bunny

You know that special time of year? Chocolate is hidden, candy is tucked away in drawers and cupboards . . . No I'm not talking about the pre-swimsuit dieting season, I'm talking about Easter time! Whatever traditions and beliefs your family has, I'm guessing that you participate in some type of deception with your children from time to time throughout the year.

I used to be troubled by this. I wondered if all the tricks and deceptions would have some long-lasting negative effects on my daughter, something that she would have to talk to her therapist about years from now. Then, all of her problems will be summed up in one sentence, "It's all your mom's fault."

To counter this, I tried to help her distinguish fact from fiction. We played "real or pretend," where I mentioned a character and she said "real" or "pretend." One day I asked her, "Tooth Fairy, real or pretend?" She rolled her eyes and said, "Oh, I know that one, Mom. It's just a guy dressed up like a fairy."

Of course this wasn't true, unless my husband is up to something I'm not aware of. Then we will all have to see a therapist. That response made me decide to quit playing "real or pretend" with her.

She obviously still wanted to believe that fairies exchange teeth for money and giant bunnies hide chocolate eggs. I decided to enjoy the innocence of her childhood for as long as I could, and I have to admit that I really enjoy playing my role in these traditions, too. But why does it have to be limited to special occasions? If you're familiar with "Random Acts of Kindness" you're familiar with this concept. That's not what we call it at our house, though. When I'm buying little treats at the store and my kids ask who they're for, I just say that I'm "being the bunny." They know what I'm talking about.

I figure, why not spread a little magic every day? Anonymously send coffee and doughnuts (or bagels) to a customer's office; hide a dollar in the sand at the playground; send flowers to those ladies at the coffee shop who greet you cheerfully after you've been up all night working on a project (and probably look like it!). Bring chocolate eggs to the workers at the copy center who finished that rush job for you ahead of time. Surprise the postman with a treat. I'm sure you are in contact with many people every day, those who could use a lift and those who help make your day a little easier. The treats and surprises don't have to be expensive, and you'll find that it's a lot of fun for you, too.

And I benefit, too. I realize that I have more energy to devote to my business and I'm more motivated in general when I spread the joy around.

Give it a try today—be the bunny!

MONEY MAKING

Telecommuting

If you want to work at home, but don't necessarily want to start a home business, telecommuting may be for you. Partly because of the current tight labor market and partly because telecommuting has proven to increase productivity and employee morale, employers are becoming more open to allowing employees to work at home.

If you want to telecommute, start with your local classified ads. Concentrate first on your skills; don't just look for ads that advertise "work at home," because they are often scams. Look for jobs that fit your experience. Employers may be open to letting you work at home, or letting you work in their offices at first and gradually move toward a telecommuting arrangement, even if they don't specifically say so in the ad. It doesn't hurt to ask. If you're online, there are also many websites that list telecommuting jobs. WAHM.com has a section devoted to telecommuting with links to job listings and the best job search sites.

All of the typical issues associated with working at home apply to telecommuters, too—only now you also have an employer to answer to. It's important to be available and accountable to your employer. Always answer your phone in a professional manner and schedule regular meetings with your employer to track your progress. Perhaps having written goals when you begin will provide checkpoints. Communication is the key. Just because you are "out of sight," don't let yourself become "out of mind."

TIP!

A Gift for You

I dreaded the first Halloween after my daughter was diagnosed with diabetes. I was afraid that one of her favorite holidays would become just another occasion for sadness, a reminder of everything she couldn't have.

When you think about it, candy is a big part of a lot of our holidays: chocolate eggs at Easter, candy canes at Christmas—but on the sugar-scale, nothing compares to Halloween.

That first post-diagnosis Halloween, we made an arrangement. I agreed to buy all of her trick-or-treating candy at the rate of 10 cents per piece. Nicki had always enjoyed trick-or-treating, but she was never willing to stay out for too long. I thought I was pretty safe with my 10 cent deal.

Because of bad weather, there weren't many trick-or-treaters out that year; everyone had extra candy. She made sure everyone knew about our arrangement and the neighbors were more than happy to oblige. They threw handfuls of candy into Nicki's bag, and told her to come back again on her way home. She went after candy like never before.

THESE DAYS WHEN PEOPLE TELL ME I HAVE A CERTAIN "GLOW" ABOUT ME, I KNOW IT'S NOT FROM PREGNANCY.

She came home with almost 15 pounds of candy, and I came home $40 lighter.

She was motivated because she had a new goal. She wasn't just going after candy, she was on a mission, a mission to set a new candy-collection record.

If you feel like you're in a rut with your business, try setting a new goal for yourself. Make it something concrete, like a dollar sales amount or a new traffic level for your website. Write down how you're going to reach your goal and schedule a realistic time frame to accomplish it.

To keep yourself on track, set up a weekly meeting with yourself or with another WAHM. See if you're on schedule to reach your goal and decide if you need to make adjustments. Another great idea is to keep a working journal. Write about what you've accomplished and how you've achieved it. You might include both your home and business life. Writing our thoughts on paper often helps to clarify ideas and solutions.

Now that you have your goal, and a plan to reach it, you need incentive. When we're working by ourselves, we don't receive the typical awards often used as incentives in the traditional workplace. Why not buy yourself a gift certificate? Choose your favorite store, buy a certificate, write "congratulations!" on the envelope and put it away until you reach your goal.

I've got a certificate to Macy's waiting for me in my filing cabinet, and I'm close to reaching my goal. Tell your friends about this book. I will thank you, and Lenore in cosmetics will really thank you.

Better Than Sex

From my personal experience, and from what I've heard from other work-at-home moms, nothing compares to the thrill of getting that first big home business check in the mail. Not sex, chocolate . . . well chocolate comes close, but it still doesn't equal the feeling of earning money from our own businesses.

I don't think it's just the money. Of course, that's great, too, but I think money serves as a validation of our businesses. After waiting for months (or years) to see a profit, finally making some decent money tells us that maybe this will all work out after all. One mom I know was so excited with her first big check that when the ice cream man drove down her street, she treated the whole neighborhood to ice cream.

My children seem to have the same entrepreneurial streak in them. I'm not sure if it's genetic, or if they're learning by example, but they're already starting businesses, too. Their favorite place to shop has become the office supply store. They love to find new pens and markers, papers, and business cards. And they love to raid my office supplies at home. My five-year-old's favorite tool is the big stapler we bought for her. It's adjustable so you can staple large pieces of paper into books or booklets. She brought it home and immediately started writing books, *The Guy on the Farm*, *Where Are My Socks?*, and my favorite, *A Dog Does Whatever It Wants To*.

When she was finished, she said, "Okay, now let's go to Barnes and Noble." I wondered why, and she said, "I have to tell them to make room on the shelves so they can sell my books!"

Oh brother, I guess the entrepreneurial acorn doesn't fall far from the tree. Who knows, with such a big head start, she just might make a go of it. So be watching for *A Dog Does Whatever It Wants To* coming soon to a book store near you, and I'll be watching the mailbox for her royalty checks.

Barter

Remember when you were a kid, and your neighbor worked your lemonade stand with you? And you paid her, not with cash, but with all the lemonade she could drink? You can still do the same thing. It's called barter and it's being used more and more today by business people.

For example, if you're an accountant, offer your services to a house cleaner in exchange for her cleaning time. Or if you clean houses, offer to clean your accountant's home and/or office in exchange for her doing your taxes. Or pay for advertising with your products instead of cash. Trade occasional child care with another WAHM when you have a client meeting or need uninterrupted work time. You will be surprised how many people are open to bartering, and it never hurts to ask.

There are many bartering clubs that you can join. By using a club, you don't have to barter directly with another businessperson whose services you want to use. The club keeps track of the services you have provided to other club members, either through "barter bucks" or some other method. You can spend your "barter bucks" with any of the other club members.

There are tax implications with bartering, because the IRS considers products and services you receive as a result of barter to be income. Be sure to check with your accountant about keeping track.

TIP!

Report Card Time

We all know them. Mothers who display their children's awards, test scores, and report cards like mounted hunting trophies on their walls and refrigerators. Our kids need to know we're proud of them, but where do we draw the line? I say we mothers deserve some recognition, too. Something more than just a Sunday in May when we receive a card and potted petunia, please.

Now, it's report card time again. How long has it been since you received a report card?

If you're working at home, you are probably dealing with many challenges.

Business issues, deadlines, and lean times. Family issues, from non-supportive spouses to sick kids and family squabbles.

But you've kept at it. You are the one who is with your children all day, and you know better than anyone else does what is best for them. You've dealt with the criticism and complaints. You've been there when your kids needed you, and you're building a business at the same time. You are the model for the new workplace, the mothers of the future.

It's about time you received a little recognition. Give yourself a pat on the back. Print out the great emails or reviews you've received, reread the notes your kids have written to you, think about all of your accomplishments: your business success, the money you've saved, the time you've spent with your family. Better yet, give yourself a report card. Give yourself a big A+. Take down one or two of the kids' pictures and hang your report card on the refrigerator. The kids won't mind and you deserve it!

Do you ever get down in the dumps? How do you stay motivated?

Working at home and taking care of kids is such a big job that I sometimes get de-motivated when I just think of all the work I need to finish! Staying up late or getting up early, along with a huge cup of coffee, usually cures that. But more important, the flexibility of owning my own business allows me to pick and choose projects that truly interest me. I always have tons more ideas than time and resources to complete them. So, I am careful to choose those things that will keep me motivated so I will actually follow through. Not only that, I know that in order to get paid, I must complete my projects and make new ventures succeed—being able to put food on the table and pay my bills is probably the biggest motivator of all!

Every so often, I have to set the alarm, get up, shower, and get dressed to pretend I'm going to work outside the home (maybe three times a year.) Those are the days that make me grateful to be home the other 362 days of the year. I would much rather burn the midnight oil at home with my home business work than put on stockings, squeeze into that old blue suit, go sit in traffic, and pay to park.

I stay motivated by surrounding myself with positive people who want great success. In addition, I take advantage of training. I listen to motivational training class daily; I watch training tapes one to three times per week from my home and I attend at least one training per month.

I think of the following:
- *The absolutely wonderful times I've been able to have with my kids since I've been home.*
- *Doing work that I love for clients I (mostly) like.*
- *How much money I'm making.*
- *How much freedom I have, both for work and for home.*
- *How unhappy I was working in an office with my kids in child care.*
- *How much time I have to talk to my husband.*
- *How guilt is not an operative word in my life anymore. (Except for eating too much!)*
- *How I got what I wanted when I really put my mind to it.*

The Work at Home Mom's Guide to Home Business

I have a "dream collage" right inside my planner. It has visuals of my goals: my dream house, college for my kids, being happy with how I spend my life, and investing for my future. I cut pictures and words from magazines that represent my goals and dreams. Glancing at this "dream collage" helps remind my why I'm working and helps me focus and stay motivated.

If I need to unwind, I do. I'll go to lunch with a friend, go shopping by myself, go antiquing with a friend. We really just like to find those little antique stores and browse, and maybe buy a little. Or I'll do something extra special with the kids.

Motivation is easy. I'm a single mom who homeschools and I have a ton of bills. Whenever I start to lose my motivation, I think about how much money I need to get by and that sure lights a fire under me.

CHAPTER ELEVEN

How Do You Spell Success?

We all have different expectations when we start a home business. Whether you dream of riches, free time, fame, or fortune, you might be surprised by how your definition of success changes over the course of your business.

New Year's Resolutions

I love January. I love the feeling of having a clean slate, a fresh start. Like many people, I write a list of resolutions at the beginning of each year and put them away until the end of the year. Then I pull them out again to see how I did. The resolutions are typically of the "lose weight, eat right, exercise, make money" variety. And, typically, I don't come close to reaching my high January expectations.

I also ask WAHM.com readers to share their resolutions each year, promising to return at the end of the year for a progress report. My favorite follow-up response was from a mom in Virginia who resolved to lose 20 pounds and make more money in her business. When I asked her how she had done, she wrote back:

"I gained twenty pounds and made less money than I had the year before. Now I'm depressed. Thanks a lot."

I'm sorry I reminded her, but, after all, it was her resolution.

Usually, when I think about motivation and resolutions, I think, "plan for success, then work the plan!" But as I was writing this, I asked my little girl what her New Year's Resolution would be. She seemed confused, so I told her:

"Think about the one thing you would like to be able to do this year. For example, you might have a goal of learning to write your ABCs. Tell me anything you can think of that you want to do this year."

She thought for a while longer and finally she said, "This year, I would like to . . . eat more candy!"

Now, the more I think about it, I think we get enough of the "work your plan!" advice. We all know that we need to work, and work hard, if we want to be successful. What we need to hear more is, "enjoy the journey." I may never reach that skinny, wealthy "paradise" of my dreams, but I can learn to enjoy each step of the journey. I was reminded of the John Lennon lyric about life happening while we're making other plans.

This year, I decided to take my resolutions a little less seriously. I'll tell more jokes and splash in the tub more, and not just at New Year's, but every day. I took out my list of resolutions, crossed everything out, and wrote "EAT MORE CANDY!" across the page.

I felt great and I'm sure our dentist will appreciate it, too.

GETTING DOWN TO BUSINESS

Financing Your Business

If you feel like you've reached a plateau but you want to continue to grow your business, it may be time to seek financing. If you didn't create a formal business plan before, you have to now. There are many resources online and in bookstores to help you through this process. The American Express Small Business Exchange even offers an online business plan tutorial, accompanied by an interactive tool to create your own plan: www.americanexpress.com/smallbusiness.

The U.S. Small Business Administration offers a variety of loan programs, including Micro Loans, which range from $100 to a maximum of $25,000.

You can learn about their loan programs and download forms from their website:www.sba.gov/financing.

You can also apply for business financing at your bank or credit union. Banks have many lending programs for small businesses and they will be happy to explain your options to you.

If you're tempted to use credit cards to finance your business, do so with caution. Carefully calculate the interest you will pay and make sure it won't overwhelm you.

Friends and family members who believe in your business may be a source of financing. Be sure to draw up a formal contract with them so there will be no misunderstanding about the terms of your loan and its repayment.

Big, Bigger, ???

"I don't think you have to chase success, but you do need to slow down enough to let it catch up to you."—Richard Carlson, *Don't Worry Make Money*

There is a trend within my peer group to drive bigger and bigger vehicles. It is not unusual to see a caravan of trucks lined up each morning, heading down the road to school. It's reminiscent of the *Smokey and the Bandit* days. All we have to do is give everyone a CB, a handle, and we got us a convoy!

Do you feel the pressure in your home business, too? Do you feel you have to continue to grow to be successful? Do you feel like you're not giving your all to your business unless you take on every project that comes your way?

THIS YEAR I RESOLVE TO:
1. LOSE 50 POUNDS
2. MAKE A MILLION DOLLARS
3. BE PATIENT AND CHEERFUL AT ALL TIMES
4. SET REALISTIC GOALS

I have a secret for work-at-home moms: bigger isn't necessarily better. I know you may not read this advice in business magazines or books, but we work-at-home moms are already breaking the traditional business rules anyway.

If you are starting to feel stressed, like you're being pulled in too many directions at once, I say it's time to take a break. Take a moment, step back, and rethink your priorities. You may find that it's time to say, "I don't need more right now." Recognize when it's time to say no to a new project. Sometimes good enough is good enough.

If you're happy with the income you're making, your current workload, and the hours you devote to your business, leave well enough alone. You have to consider what expanding could mean to the time that you have to spend with your family, your children, and husband.

So remember, bigger isn't always better. Heck, even Pamela Lee had her implants removed.

How do you define success?

I feel that my business is a success because I'm able to stay home with my kids, pay the bills, and still have enough left over to pay for piano lessons for my daughter. That's all I ask for.

I will feel successful when a publisher asks me to write a series of books.

I dream of going on a book tour and also leading women's retreats and conferences. I know it will happen, it's just a matter of when it will happen.

I feel successful now. I am doing what I love to do. I feel that I have found my calling.

I first felt that my business was a success when I was named one of the top regional saleswomen in my company.

I will be a success when someone calls offering to buy my business for a ton of money, and I will politely tell them, "it's not for sale!"

When I see my paintings hanging in a gallery surrounded by wealthy art patrons who are all getting out their checkbooks.

I felt my business was a success when a friend introduced me as "my friend, the business owner."

My success was defined the day my teenage daughter told me "I'm so glad you're home Mom", My teenager!

CHAPTER TWELVE

And Finally...

I'm always learning new things and being inspired by other WAHMs. I hope this advice will help you too, both now and in the future.

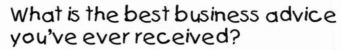

What is the best business advice you've ever received?

Never forget the reason you started this business in the first place—your kids.

This quote from Harvey Mackay: "Time is precious. You can't own it, but you can use it. You can't keep it, but you can spend it. Once you've lost it, you can never get it back."

Two things: Do what you do best, and do what you love. There have been so many times I've wanted to give up, but had it not been for those two reasons, I would have done so already! Because, then I would ask myself, "Well, what if I got a 'real' job, what would it be?" Answer: I would want to be doing the same thing, except I would be working for someone else!

To keep my priorities straight and not get bogged down in the details.

The best thing I have learned is the fact that it doesn't have to be done all in one day. Having a business has taught me how to pace myself. It's also taught me that when a person tries to shoot me down, I am capable of brushing off their negativity and working on. That's a skill I never thought I had until I started a business.

This quote from Helen Keller: "Life is a daring adventure, or nothing at all."

This is my philosophy on starting and running my home-based business. Just be myself; friendly and honest. And if I concentrate on giving, the getting will take care of itself!

Don't give up. And feel free to hang up on all those "friends" who interrupt you with phone calls, because after all, you're home all day!

One of the best things I've learned is also very simple.

Don't try to reinvent the wheel. Find those who are having the level of success that you want, and do what they did. Of course, you do have to make tiny modifications based on your own style and personality. Don't worry that you might model yourself after someone who is unethical—those people don't last. Find someone who has been at it for awhile and simply do what he or she did. Success leaves clues!

My Advice to All WAHMs

WAHMs . . . don't stuff envelopes.
If I can offer you only one tip, this is it.

No one will pay you $3 to lick an envelope, never have, never will.

Now, the rest of my advice.
Enjoy your kids. Trust me, in 20 years they will be gone. Their handprints will still be on your walls, but the pitter-patter of little feet will be a distant memory.

Don't worry about your business; or worry, but know that worrying is as effective as trying to get connected to the Internet by making modem sounds into your phone. The real troubles in your business are apt to pop up at 4 a.m. when in a sleep-deprived fog you accidentally send a *very* personal love letter to 100 of your clients.

Make one new contact every day.

Back up the hard drive on your computer or you'll miss it when it's gone.

Maybe you'll make it, maybe you won't, maybe you'll be back to the old 9 to 5 job, maybe you'll dance the funky chicken when your company goes public and you make a bundle on stock options.

Shower.

Do NOT read Martha Stewart's magazine. It will only make you feel inadequate.

Get to know your computer repair technicians; you never know when you'll need them at 5:30 p.m. on a Friday evening.

Be good to your modem. It is your link to the world.

Accept certain inalienable truths:

- your neighbor will never accept the fact that you "work."
- your kids will never enjoy cauliflower.
- your husband will never willingly wash the dishes.
- your kids will grow up, they'll have kids of their own, and you will fantasize that when your kids were little, you never let them eat Fruit Loops for dinner.

When you do someone a favor, don't expect one in return. If someone does something nice for you, you must return the favor.

Be careful who you listen to. If you really want to be home with your kids, you can probably find a way to do it. Remember, not everyone has your best interests in mind. No one can give you all the answers. Listen to your heart.

But trust me on the envelopes.

Appendix A
Work-at-Home Ideas

Accountant

Advertising sales

Advertising design

Antique and
collectibles dealer
(check out the online
auctions such as
www.ebay.com,
auctions.yahoo.com and
auctions.amazon.com)

Apartment locator

Artist

Astrologer

Baby announcements

Balloon sculpture/
animal creator

Bookkeeper

Book publishing

Book sales

Bridal services

Business brochure design

Business card printing

Cartoonist

Caterer

Child care

Clothing design

Clothing sales

Clown

Computer tutor/classes

Computer consulting

Computer programming

Computer setup
and repair

Convention planner

Cosmetics sales

Costume sewing
(local theaters,
historical sites,
Halloween)

Custom tailor

Database design

Data entry

Decorative painting
(murals, faux finishes)

Desktop publishing

Direct sales
(See appendix B)

Doctor

Doll designer

Editor

Engineer
(Check local want
ads for contract
engineering positions)

Face painter

Feng-Shui consultant

Foreign language classes/
instructor

Furniture design/
decorating

Ghost writer

Gift baskets

Gift bouquets
(candy, cookie)

Graphic design

Greeting card design

Greeting card writer

Hair stylist

Holiday letters
(personalized Happy
Birthday letters,
letters from Santa,
the Easter Bunny)

Horoscope columnist

Housekeeping

Illustrator

Image consultant

Interior design

Internet promotion

Internet sales

Investigator

Jewelry design

Mail order sales

Medical billing

Medical transcription

Merchandiser

Money management

Museum display design
and sales

Newsletter publisher

Party planner

Party product sales

Personal coach

Personal shopper

Personal trainer

Pet grooming

Pet sitting

Photographer

Pinata maker
(customized for
individuals and parties)

Portrait painter

Private investigator

Professional organizer
(home and office)

Proofreader

Promotional
product sales

Psychic readings

Public relations

Puppy day camp

Radio program

Real estate
(sales and consulting)

Reminder service

Secretarial services

Security products/
services

Sew fantasy costumes for
children's portraits

Shopping services

Sign maker

Small business coach

Special event planner

Stock photographer

Storyteller

Technical writer

Therapist

Translation services

Travel agent

Tutor

Website designer

Website publisher

Wedding planner/
Consultant

Writer

Yard sign sales
(baby announcements)

Appendix B:
Direct Sales Companies

If you're considering direct sales, here are some companies to choose from. You can either contact a representative in your area, or use the contact information below. If a national phone number isn't listed, check your local phone listing for a distributor near you.

Most of these companies are members of the Direct Selling Association as of January 1, 2000. As members, they have pledged to abide by the DSA'a Code of Ethics as a condition of admission and continuing membership. Visit the Direct Selling Association's website (www.dsa.org) to learn more.

The other companies I've included are smaller and/or fairly new. I've found them to have high quality products.

1-800-Party Shop*
800 party shop
www.1800partyshop.com
Person-to-Person

Achievers Unlimited, Inc.
Nutritional Products
561-835-3777
www.achieversunltd.com
Person-to-Person

Act II Jewelry
800-487-3323
www.ladyremingtonjewelry.com
Party Plan

AdvoCare
Weight Management
  Products, Skincare
214:831-1033
Person-to-Person

Aloette Cosmwahm.com
Skincare, Cosmetics,
  Fragrances
1-800-ALOETTE
www.aloettecosmetics.com
Party Plan

Arbonne International, Inc.
Skincare, Cosmetics,
  Nutritional Products
1-800-ARBONNE
www.arbonne.com
Party Plan and
  Person-to-Person

AIM U.S.A.
Nutritional Products
800-456-2462
www.theaimcompanies.com
Person-to-Person

AMC Corporation
Cookware, Multi-Cooking
  Systems
www.amcint.com
Party Plan

**American Communications
Network, Inc. (ACN)**
Long Distance Service,
  Debit Calling Card,
  Pay Phones,Telecom-
  munications Services
810-528-2500
Person-to-Person

Amora International, LC
Skincare
888-802-6672
www.amoraskincare.com
Person-to-Person

Amway Corporation
Homecare Products, Home
  Technology Products,
  Nutritional Products,
  Personal Care Products,
  Commercial Products/
  Services
www.amway.com
Person-to-Person

Art Finds International, Inc.
Art
317-248-2666
Party Plan

Artistic Impressions, Inc.
Art
630-916-0050
Party Plan

Assured Nutrition Plus
Nutritional Products,
    Weight Management
    Products
937-548-7713
Party Plan and
    Person-To-Person

Avon Products, Inc.
Cosmetics, Decorative
    Accessories, Giftware,
    Jewelry, Skincare, Toys/
    Games, Nutritional
    Products
800-367-2866
www.avon.com
Person-to-Person

**BeautiControl
Cosmetics, Inc.**
Cosmetics, Skincare,
    Nutritional Products,
    Image Services
800-232-8841
www.beauticontrol.com
Party Plan

**Beverly Sassoon
and Company***
Skin Care, Dietary and
    Sports Nutritional
    Supplements
www.bsassoon.net
Person-to-Person

big enough*
Women and children's
    Cotton Sportswear
800-288-7321
www.bigenough.com
Party Plan and
    Person-To-Person

**Body Wise
International, Inc.**
Nutritional Products
800-830-9596
www.bodywise.com
Person-to-Person

Carico International, Inc.
Cookware, Water Treatment
    Systems, Juice Extractor,
    China, Crystal, Cutlery,
    Tableware, Air Filters
954-973-3900
Party Plan and
    Person-To-Person

Changes International, Inc.
Nutritional Products
800-933-7424
www.changesinternational.com
Person-to-Person

Charmelle
Jewelry
800-846-5393
www.charmelle.com
Party Plan and
    Person-To-Person

**Colesce Couture
International**
Lingerie/Sleepwear
214-631-4860
www.colesce.com
Party Plan

Color Me Beautiful
Cosmetics, Skincare
703-471-6400
www.colorme.com
Party Plan and
    Person-To-Person

Conklin Company, Inc.
Personal Care Products,
    Homecare Products
800-888-8838
www.conklin.com
Party Plan and
    Person-To-Person

**Cookin' the American Way
(Division of House of Lloyd)**
Cookware
800-733-2465
www.catw.com
Party Plan

**Country Peddlers &
Company of America, Inc.**
Decorative Accessories
800-873-3537
www.cpca-usa.com
Party Plan

Creative Memories
Photo Albums, Photo
    Album Supplies
800-468-9335
www.creative-memories.com
Party Plan

CUTCO/Vector Corporation
Cutlery
800-828-0448
www.cutco.com
Person-to-Person

Discovery Toys, Inc.
Toys/Games, Books, Child
    care Products, Educa-
    tional Materials, Videos
800-426-4777
www.discoverytoysinc.com
Party Plan

DK Family Learning
Books, Videos
800-352-6651
www.dk.com
Party Plan and
    Person-To-Person

Doncaster
Clothing, Fashion
    Accessories
800-669-3662
www.doncaster.com
Person-to-Person

DS-MAX U.S.A. Inc.
Books, Business Products,
    Plants/Foliage, Toys/
    Games, Giftware, House
    and Kitchenwares
714-587-9207
Person-to-Person

Dudley Products, Inc.
Cosmetics, Fragrances,
    Skincare, Haircare
800-334-4150
www.dudleyq.com
Person-to-Person

**Eagle Distributing
Company, Inc.**
Fire alarms/extinguishers,
    "Child Finder"
    Window Decals

800-825-5880
www.homefiresafety.com
Person-to-Person

Electrolux Corporation
Vacuum Cleaners,
    Homecare Products
800-243-9078
www.electrolux-usa.com
Person-to-Person

Enrich International
Health/Fitness Products,
    Skincare
801-226-2600
www.enrich.com
Party Plan and
    Person-To-Person

ENVION International
Nutritional Products,
    Personal Care Products
800-436-8466
www.envion.com
Person-to-Person

Enviro-Tech International
Autocare Products, Personal
    Care Products, Ani-
    malcare Products/Food,
    Nutritional Products
702-262-5544
www.enviro-tech.com
Person-to-Person

Equinox International
Water Treatment Systems,
    Air Filters, Nutritional
    Products, Skincare, Cos-
    metics, Haircare, Personal
    Care Products, Homecare
    Products, Weight Man-
    agement Products
800-777-2777.
www.equinoxinternational.com
Person-to-Person

**Essentially Yours
Industries Corp.**
Nutritional Products,
    Weight Management
    Products
604-596-9766
Person-to-Person

Excel Communications, Inc.
Long Distance Service
800-875-9235
www.excel.com
Person-to-Person

ForYou, Inc.
Skincare, Self-improvement
Programs
843-756-9000
Party Plan and
Person-To-Person

FreeLife International
Nutritional Products,
Skincare
203-882-7250
www.freelifeonline.com
Person-to-Person

The Fuller Brush Company
Homecare Products,
House and Kitchenwares,
Personal Care Products
316-792-1711
www.fullerbrush.com
Person-to-Person

Golden Neo-Life Diamite International
Nutritional Products,
Homecare Products,
Skincare, Water Treat-
ment Systems,Weight
Management Products
800-432-5848
www.gnld.com
Person-to-Person

Golden Pride International
Nutritional Products,
Weight Management
Products, Health/Fitness
Products, House and
Kitchenwares, Water
Treatment Systems,
Food/Beverage Products,
Skincare
561-640-5700
www.goldenpride.com
Person-to-Person

The Good Nature Company
Bird feeding products,
garden accessories
248-628-4103
Party Plan

Henn Workshops
Decorative Accessories
330-824-2575
www.hennworkshops.com
Party Plan

Herbalife International
Weight Management
Products, Nutritional
Products, Personal Care
Products, Fragrances
310-216-9661
www.herbalife.com
Person-to-Person

Highlights for Children, Inc.
Educational Materials
614-486-0631
Person-to-Person

Holbrook Cottage, Inc.
Home Accessories, Gifts,
Gourmet Foods
914-944-0734
Party Plan

Home & Garden Party, Inc.
Pottery, Art, Decorative
Accessories
800-700-7873
www.homeandgardenparty.com
Party Plan

Home Interiors & Gifts, Inc.
Decorative Accessories,
Giftware
972-386-1000
www.homeinteriors.com
Party Plan

The Homemakers Idea Company (Wicker World Enterprises)
Decorative Accessories
800-800-5452
www.thehomemakersideaco.com
Party Plan

House of Lloyd, Inc.
Christmas Decorations,
Giftware, Decorative
Accessories, Toys/Games
800-733-2465
www.catw.com
Party Plan

Hsin Ten Enterprise USA, Inc.
Health/Fitness Products
www.hteusa.com
Party Plan and
 Person-to-Person

Hy Cite Corporation
Cookware, Water Treatment
 Systems, Air Purification
 Crystal/China, Cutlery
608-663-0600
www.royalprestige.com
Party Plan and
 Person-to-Person

I-Link Worldwide, LLC
Long Distance Service
800-368-3038
www.i-linkww.net
Person-to-Person

Integris International, Inc.
Nutritional Products
888-737-7307
www.integriscorp.com
Person-to-Person

Interior Design Nutritionals (Division of Nu Skin International)
Nutritional Products,
 Weight Management
 Products
800-487-1500
www.nuskin.com
Person-to-Person

Interstate Engineering
Vacuum Cleaners
714-758-5011
Person-to-Person

Jafra Cosmetics International, Inc.
Skincare, Cosmetics,
 Fragrances
800-551-2345
www.jafra.com
Party Plan and
 Person-to-Person

Jeunique International, Inc.
Cosmetics,
 Lingerie/Sleepwear,
 Nutritional Products,
 Skincare

909-598-8598
Party Plan and
 Person-to-Person

Kelly's Kids, Inc.
Children's clothing
800-370-9221
www.kellyskids.com
Party Plan

Kids Only Clothing Club, Inc.
Clothing
403-252-9667
Party Plan

The Kirby Company
Vacuum Cleaners
www.kirby.com
Person-to-Person

Kitchen Fair (Regal Ware, Inc.)
Cookware, Decorative
 Accessories, House
 and Kitchenwares
501-982-0555
Party Plan

Kizure Products Company, Inc.
Haircare
310-604-0032
Person-to-Person

Learning Wonders
Educational Material
800-537-7227
www.learningwonders.com
Party Plan

Legacy Health International, Inc.
Nutritional Products
516-942-3462
Person-to-Person

Legacy USA, Inc.
Nutritional Products
407-951-8815
Person-to-Person

LifeLink LLC
Nutritional Products,
 Personal Care Products
208-525-7850
Person-to-Person

LifeScience Technologies, Ltd.
Nutritional Products,
    Personal Care Products,
    Telecommunications
    Services, Prepaid Calling
    Cards, Long Distance
    Service
www.lifesciencetech.com
Person-to-Person

The Longaberger Company
Decorative Accessories,
    House and Kitchenwares
800-966-0374
www.longaberger.com
Party Plan

Longevity Network, Ltd.
Nutritional Products,
    Skincare, Haircare,
    Personal Care Products
800-242-1000
www.longevitynetwork.com
Person-to-Person

Magnus Enterprises, Inc.
Nutritional Products,
    Cosmetics
310-532-8440
Party Plan and
    Person-to-Person

Mannatech, Inc.
Nutritional Products
888-346-4636
www.mannatech-inc.com
Person-to-Person

Market America, Inc.
Personal Care Products,
    Nutritional Products,
    Homecare Products,
    Autocare Products,
    Photography
336-605-0040
www.marketamericausa.com
Person-to-Person

Mary Kay Inc.
Cosmetics, Skincare
www.marykay.com
Party Plan and
    Person-to-Person

Masterguard Corporation
Fire Alarms/Extinguisher
972-446-9966
www.masterguard.com
Party Plan and
    Person-to-Person

Melaleuca, Inc.
Nutritional Products,
    Personal Care Products,
    Homecare Products
800-742-2444
www.melaleuca.com
Person-to-Person

Millennium Direct Marketing, Inc.
Nutritional Products,
    Skincare
417-781-9995
www.stopaging.com
Party Plan and
    Person-to-Person

Morinda, Inc.
Nutritional Products,
    Noni Juice
800-445-2969
www.morinda.com
Person-to-Person

Muscle Dynamics Fitness Network, Inc.
Health/Fitness Products,
    Nutritional Products,
    Weight Management
    Products
310-715-8036
Person-to-Person

The Nationwide Companies
Benefits Packages, jewelry,
    nutritional products,
    telecommunications,
    automobiles
800-273-2517
www.nationwideautoclub.com
Person-to-Person

Nature's Own
Skincare, Nutritional
    Products, Health/Fitness
    Products
203-380-8900
Person-to-Person

wahm.com

APPENDIX

B

Nest Entertainment, Inc.
Bible Video Tapes, Videos,
   Audio Tapes,
   Educational Materials
800-973-6378
www.nestentertainment.com
Party Plan and
   Person-to-Person

Network America, Inc.
Group Buying Service
972-756-0644
Party Plan and
   Person-to-Person

**New Image
International, Inc.**
Weight Management Prod-
   ucts, Nutritional Products
502-867-1895
www.newimageint.com
Person-to-Person

**New Vision
International, Inc.**
Nutritional Products,
   Personal Care Products,
   Skincare and Sports
   Supplements, Weight
   Management Products
800-646-3725
www.nviworld.com
Person-to-Person

Nikken, Inc.
Bedding Products,
   Nutritional Products
www.nikken.com
Party Plan and
   Person-to-Person

Noevir USA, Inc.
Skincare, Cosmetics,
   Nutritional Products
800-872-8817
www.noevirusa.com
Person-to-Person

NSA
Air Filters, Water
   Treatment Systems,
   Educational Materials,
   Nutritional Products
www.nsanet.com/
   welcome.html
Person-to-Person

Nu Skin International, Inc.
Haircare, Nutritional
   Products, Skincare
800-487-1500
www.nuskin.com
Party Plan and
   Person-to-Person

Nutri-Metics International, Inc.
Skincare, Homecare Prod-
   ucts, Nutritional Products
Party Plan

**Nutrition For Life
International, Inc.** *
Nutritional Products,
   Weight Management
   Products, Skincare, Long
   Distance Service, Internet
   Advertising Services,
   Homeopathics
800-344-5892
www.nutritionforlife.com
Person-to-Person

Oriflame U.S.A.
Skincare, Cosmetics,
   Fragrances, Nutritional
   Products
800-959-0699
Person-to-Person

Oxyfresh Worldwide, Inc.
Dental Hygiene, Skincare,
   Animalcare Products/
   Food, Nutritional
   Products,Haircare,
   Homecare Products,
   Personal Care Products
800-223-7374
www.oxyfreshworldwide.com
Person-to-Person

The Pampered Chef, Ltd.
House and Kitchenwares,
   Cookware
800-266-5562
www.pamperedchef.com
Party Plan

Pangea, Ltd.
Nutritional Products,
   Skincare
770-998-9181
Person-to-Person

PartyLite Gifts, Inc.
Candles, Candle Accessories
www.partylite.com
Party Plan

Petra Fashions, Inc.
Lingerie/Sleepwear
978-777-5853
www.petra4u.com
Party Plan

Pola U.S.A., Inc.
Skincare, Cosmetics,
    Haircare, Fragrances
310-527-9696
Party Plan and
    Person-to-Person

Premier Designs, Inc.
Jewelry
800-486-7378
www.premierdesigns.com
Party Plan and
    Person-to-Person

Primerica Financial Services
Financial/Investment
    Services, Insurance
www.pfsnet.com
Person-to-Person

Princess House, Inc.
Decorative Accessories,
    Crystal/China, Jewelry
800-622-0039
www.princesshouse.com
Party Plan

Pro-Monde Marketing, Inc.
Long Distance Service,
    Travel
www.pro-monde.com
Person-to-Person

Providence House, LLC
Catholic books and gifts
704-358-9970
Party Plan and
    Person-to-Person

**PRP Wine
International, Inc.**
Wine
847-290-7800
Person-to-Person

RACHAeL International
Skincare, Haircare, Cosmet-
    ics, Nutritional Products
800-398-2563
www.rachaelinternational.com
Party Plan and
    Person-to-Person

Regal Ware, Inc.
Cookware, Cutlery,
    Tableware, Water
    Treatment Systems
www.regalware.com
Party Plan and
    Person-to-Person

Reliv' International, Inc.
Nutritional Products,
    Personal Care Products
636-537-9715
www.reliv.com
Person-to-Person

Remember Me
Dolls, Doll Accessories
517-832-6414
Party Plan and
    Person-to-Person

**Rena-Ware
Distributors, Inc.**
Cookware
206-881-6171
Party Plan and
    Person-to-Person

Rexair, Inc.
Vacuum Cleaners,
    Homecare Products
www.rainbowsystem.com
Person-to-Person

**Rexall Showcase
International**
Health/Fitness Products,
    Nutritional Products,
    Water Treatment Systems,
    Personal Care Products
561-994-2090
www.rexallshowcase.com
Person-to-Person

Rich Plan Corporation
Food/Beverage Products,
    Home Appliances

800-662-3663
www.richplan.com
Person-to-Person

The Right Solution
Health/Fitness Products,
Nutritional Products,
Weight Management
Products
702-399-4328
Person-to-Person

Saladmaster, Inc. (Regal Ware, Inc.)
Cookware, Tableware
817-633-3555
Party Plan and
Person-to-Person

Seaborne, Inc.
Nutritional Products
877-738-0990
www.seaborne.com
Person-to-Person

Shaklee Corporation
Nutritional Products,
Personal Care Products,
Homecare Products,
Water Treatment Systems
www.shaklee.com
Person-to-Person

ShapeRite
Weight Management
Products, Personal Care
Products
888-742-7374
www.shaperite.com
Person-to-Person

The Southwestern Company
Books, Educational
Materials
615-391-2500
www.southwestern.com
Person-to-Person

Specialty Products Network
Gourmet Coffee, Meat
and Food
440-243-0088
Party Plan and
Person-to-Person

Sportron International, Inc.
Nutritional Products,
Weight Management
Products, Skincare,
Homecare Products
800-843-1202
www.sportron.net
Person-to-Person

Stampin' Up!
Rubber Stamps
800-782-6787
www.stampinup.com
Party Plan

Stanley Home Products
Homecare Products,
Personal Care Products,
Wellness Products
800-628-9032
www.stanleyhome.com
Party Plan

The Story Teller
Books, Educational
Materials, Cassettes,
Toys/Games
www.thestoryteller.com
Party Plan

Success Motivation Institute
Self-improvement Program,
Time Management
Programs
254-776-7551
www.success-motivation.com
Person-to-Person

Sunrider International
Nutritional Products,
Skincare, Personal Care
Products, Cosmetics,
Homecare Products
www.sunrider.com
Person-to-Person

SupraLife
Nutritional Products,
Skincare, Haircare,
Oral Hygiene
www.toddy.com
Party Plan and
Person-to-Person

Symmetry Corporation
Nutritional Products,
  Weight Management
  Products
www.symmcorp.com
Party Plan and
  Person-to-Person

Table Charm Corporation
Cookware, Tableware
905-470-7874
www.tablecharm.com
Person-to-Person

Tarrah
Skincare
561-640-5700
Party Plan and
  Person-to-Person

Taste of Gourmet
Food/Beverage Products
662-887-2522
www.tasteofgourmet.com
Party Plan

Tomorrow's Treasures, Inc.
Home Photography
  Workshops, Photo Lab
  Services, Enlargements,
  Processing, Personalized
  Photo Gift Items,
  Photo Display Items
800-899-5656, ext. 1099
www.tomorrowstreasures.net
Party Plan and
  Person-to-Person

Trek Alliance, Inc.
Weight Management
  Products,
  Nutritional Products,
  Skincare
www.trekalliance.com
Party Plan and
  Person-to-Person

Tupperware Corporation
House and Kitchenwares,
  Toys/Games
www.tupperware.com
Party Plan and
  Person-to-Person

Unique Solutions, Inc.
Nutritional Products, Travel,
  Air Filters, Aromatherapy
888-882-8872
www.networkusi.com
Person-to-Person

United Consumers Club, Inc.
Group Buying Service
www.shopucc.com
Person-to-Person

**U.S. Safety & Engineering
Corporation**
Security Systems/Devices
916-482-8888
Person-to-Person

USANA, Inc.
Nutritional Products,
  Skincare
801-954-7100
www.usana.com
Party Plan and
  Person-to-Person

Usborne Books at Home
Books
800-475-4522
www.ubah.com
Party Plan and
  Person-to-Person

Vantel Pearls in the Oyster
Pearls, Jewelry
508-698-2220
www.vantelpearls.com
Party Plan

Vita Craft Corporation
Cookware, Crystal/China,
  Cutlery, Tableware,
  Water Treatment Systems
913-631-6265
www.vitacraft.com
Party Plan and
  Person-to-Person

Viva America Marketing, Inc.
Nutritional Products,
  Skincare, Weight
  Management Products,
  Fitness Products
800-243-8482
www.vivalife.com
Party Plan and
  Person-to-Person

Viviane Woodard Industries, Inc.
Skincare, Cosmetics, Fragrances
800-423-3600
www.woodard.com
Person-to-Person

Vorwerk USA Company, L.P.
Food Preparation Appliances, Floor Care
407-772-2222
Party Plan

Watkins Incorporated
Nutritional Products, Personal Care Products, Food/Beverage Products, Homecare Products
507-457-3300
www.watkins-inc.com
Person-to-Person

Weekender USA, Inc.
* Clothing
www.weekenders.com
Party Plan

The West Bend Company
Cookware, Water Treatment Systems
www.westbend.com
Party Plan and Person-to-Person

Wicker Plus, Ltd.
Decorative Accessories
800-942- 5758
www.wickerplus.com
Party Plan

World Book, Inc.
Encyclopedias, Educational Materials
800-967-5325
www.worldbook.com
Person-to-Person

Youngevity, Inc.
Nutritional Products
www.youngevity.com
Person-to-Person

Yves Rocher, Inc.
Beauty Care
713-626-2255
Party Plan and Person-to-Person

Not a member of the Direct Selling Association as of 1-1-00

Appendix C
Resources Available at WAHM.com
The Online Magazine for
Work-at-Home Moms

My website, WAHM.com can be found at www.wahm.com.

The site has resources for moms (and dads) who are looking for a home business as well as those who are already working at home. In addition to my weekly column and cartoon, you will find advice from many other work-at-home experts.

Here are some of the other things you will find at WAHM.com:

Mailing Lists

Email mailing lists are available on the following topics:

- This week at WAHM.com: WAHM.com weekly newsletter.
- WAHM.com discussion list: Discuss home business issues with other work-at-home moms (and dads).
- WAHM.com chat list: On the main discussion list we talk about business; on this list, we just talk. Talk with other WAHMs about current events and issues.
- WAHM.com Fun list: Clean jokes, stories, poems, cute things the kids say.
- WAHMs who homeschool: Communicate with other WAHMs who homeschool their children.
- WAHMs in consulting and training.
- WAHM around the world: Meet WAHMs outside the United States.
- WAHMs in Canada: Canadian WAHMs communicate and talk about issues unique to their Canadian businesses.
- WAHMs who are child care operators.
- WAHMs in MLM.
- WAHMs in MT: Medical Transcription and/or Billing
- WAHMs in web design.
- WAHMs who write.

wahm.com

APPENDIX C

Mailing Lists, continued

- Grandma WAHMs
- Single WAHMs
- Crafting WAHMs
- WAHMs in party plans

Before you sign up for a mailing list, be sure to read the frequently asked questions or FAQs at www.wahm.com/listfaqs.html.

You can subscribe to the lists at www.wahm.com/lists/sub.html.

Message Boards
There are message boards covering all of the above topics and more. You'll find the message boards at www.wahm.com/cgi-bin/Ultimate.cgi.

Location Directory
Add your email address and meet and network with other WAHMs in your area through the WAHM.com location directory at www.wahm.com/directory.html.

There are listings for WAHMs all over the world.

Business Directory
You can list your business and search for other businesses in the WAHM.com business directory at www.wahm.com/business.html.

Telecommuting
New telecommuting jobs are added every day at www.wahm.com/jobs.html.

Business Opportunities
Business Opportunities are listed at www.wahm.com/opp.html.

When you're at WAHM.com, you can write to me at cheryl@wahm.com. I can't guarantee that I can personally answer each email, but I do try, and I love hearing from my readers.

What would you tell someone who's not online yet? How has WAHM.com helped you and your business?

WAHM.com is the most wonderfully supportive community I have come across on the Internet-and possibly anywhere. While there are other websites geared to groups that overlap or relate to moms who are (or who want to be) working from home, this one is the most open, helpful, and (to repeat myself) supportive. Cheryl Demas, site owner and editor, has done a terrific job creating and encouraging that atmosphere. I have made a number of friends through the mailing list and have learned a great deal from both the mailing list and the website.

I can hardly tell you how much WAHM.com has done for my family and me. I was a single mom of five, desperately poor. I had very little college, and had been out of the workplace for ten years. I was left with no marketable skills, no hopes of being able to go outside of my home and earn enough to pay child care (which I was terribly opposed to anyway) let alone take care of the mortgage, food, and other bills.

I decided that I needed to run up my debt to buy a computer to join the real world. That's when I found WAHM.com. Without the support and shared information from the ladies on the WAHM.com mailing list, I would have lost sight of my goals. Over several years, I kept seeing other moms working so hard. Some were simply surviving, some weren't even doing that. Others, though, were doing very well for their kids and themselves. I kept pushing ahead, really believing that it was there for me. What I would tell other moms considering working from home: You have to have conviction. If you just want to work from home because you feel it would be easier to be your own boss, forget it. I am much harder on myself than any boss I've ever worked for. I am a brutal slave driver. It can also be much easier dealing with coworkers than with your mini-roommates 24/7. You need to think seriously about

wahm.com

READERS

why you want to be a WAHM. If your reasons are more than, "It would be easier than..." or "It sounds like fun," then it might be for you. If you have a strong belief that you need to be earning a living at home, then don't ever lose sight of your goals. WAHM.com is about support, sharing information, fellowship: laughing and crying, prayers, congratulations and condolences.

WAHM.com has been an invaluable resource for me. I have learned so much about working from home (e.g., marketing, job searching.) The resources that are shared on the site and mailing list are also extremely helpful, from technical advice to general support. I also landed one of my biggest contracts through WAHM.com. One of the WAHMs was unable to take on an editing job for a large resource manual and posted it to the site. I submitted my information to her and she forwarded it to the employer and I was selected! The job pays my consulting wage and it has been active since November and will probably last until March. I am truly grateful for this resource.

When I first quit my job over two years ago to become a WAHM, I thought that I wouldn't miss the office atmosphere. I thought it would be more relaxing to work from home. What I found was that it was a bit isolating and although I had all day, kids or laundry or the doorbell frequently interrupted me. I have been so grateful to WAHM.com for giving me back the "water cooler." I am able to take a break now and again to converse with working moms all over who have the same challenges and goals that I do. (Try to find that at the "water cooler"!) Also I have received much enthusiastic help and advice from the other WAHMs, which has made life a bit easier and/or more productive. I have needed some technical help here and there to get my websites up or to apply for a merchant account and have been able to receive information almost instantaneously over email! This information would have taken me time to research over the web or even more time and possibly some money to find out from a so-called expert from the yellow pages. Not only did I find the information, but I also learned how it worked for another WAHM! That's value you can't get from asking a big office expert.

I am doing this on my own as my husband is only quasi supportive, not very creative, and unfamiliar with juggling motherhood and the discipline of working from home. (To a husband, juggling two things at once is watching the football game and balancing the chips and dip on his knee!) It is a blessing from God to have a forum where you can not only feel free to ask questions but to also get honest, tried and true answers without the hype. The icing on the cake is really the most precious part of WAHM.com: the friendships. I would have had to move to several different cities, states, and even countries in order to meet these wonderful ladies! How else could a WAHM from Southern California have lunch with a WAHM from Canada?

Working at home with little ones underfoot can be a challenging and sometimes isolating (although very rewarding) experience. On one level, being able to connect with other moms who are in similar situations and who care about the same things gives me a daily dose of encouragement. On another level, WAHM.com has enabled me to do research for my writing projects, find out about critical business issues such as what to charge for my services, and locate resources that can help me in my work.

I have been visiting WAHM.com now for more than three years. I have met some wonderful moms out there through WAHM.com. I love the networking and assistance offered to me as well as the opportunity to provide my two cents worth. Being a single mom of two, I know the challenges of being a mom in the workplace, at home or otherwise.

wahm.com

READERS

Appendix D
Sample Press Release

Stay Home with Your Kids Day
For Immediate Release

Date
Contact: your name here
your title
email
phone
your URL
Cheryl Demas, Publisher WAHM.com
chdemas@aol.com
(916) 985-2078
http://www.wahm.com/

Local home-based businesswoman, "**your name here**" is preparing to celebrate the fourth annual "Stay Home with Your Kids Day" on Monday August 21, 2000. Stay Home With Your Kids Day is sponsored by WAHM.com: The Online Magazine for Work at Home Moms. The purpose of the day is to encourage and support those parents who have chosen to be home with their children.

Cheryl Demas, publisher of the WAHM.com website, says "If you're thinking about leaving the traditional workplace, Stay Home with Your Kids Day is the perfect opportunity to take a vacation day and give serious thought to making the change. Leaving your job may not be an easy decision, but if your heart aches every time you drive away from the child care center in the morning, it might be time to look at other options." And there are many options for parents today, aside from working full-time outside the home. Many parents are finding that working from home is the perfect solution to their work/home dilemma.

"**Your name here**" has been running "**your business here**" from her home since "**date.**"

"**Enter additional information about your business, and/or a quote about your feelings about being a WAHM here.**"

As Demas states, "If we can have a day to take our children to work, we should be able to devote one day to staying home with our children. While we realize that not all parents can or wish to be home full-time with their kids, WAHM.com is dedicated to giving advice and support to those who are determined to make it work. Give it a try; 'Mom' can be the best job description you've ever had."

Note from Cheryl: Stay Home with Your Kids Day is observed on the third Monday in August each year.

ABOUT CHERYL

Cheryl Demas is an incredible role model for all women. She's discovered how to balance her life needs with raising a family and running a business. Cheryl lives with her husband Mike, her two daughters Nicki and Dani along with their dog Alice, in their suburban home in Folsom, California. Her energy goes into living life to the fullest, not complaining and giving back to others instead of focussing on herself.

www.wahm.com

Hear what people are saying about
WAHM.COM...

"Hot Site of the Day"
—**USA Today**

"WAHM is an exceptional resource for women whose office is at home."
—**Small Business Resource Guide to the Web/Lycos Press**

"Great support for those among us who grapple with the three-peanut-butter-sandwich lunch."
—**Women's Wire Web Directory**

Web Entrepreneuer Magazine has given WAHM.com their "Business Resource Award" which is given to websites that "demonstrate substantial utility to entrepreneurs and business leaders."

Readers comments:
"Erma Bombeck on the Internet"

"You've helped so many of us who have dreamed of owning our own business and are now making it a reality."

"I read through all your columns this morning. You had me laughing and crying in my coffee . . . Thank you!"

"This book offers a realistic insight on what working-at-home is all about. No fluff. Just the nitty gritty on the day-to-day life of a work-at-home mom."

www.wahm.com

Your Notes on Starting
Your Work-at-Home Business

www.wahm.com

Your Notes on Starting
Your Work-at-Home Business

www.wahm.com